Synonyms and Antonyms

BY
DEBORAH WHITE BROADWATER

COPYRIGHT © 2001 Mark Twain Media, Inc.

ISBN 1-58037-161-2

Printing No. CD-1382

Mark Twain Media, Inc., Publishers
Distributed by Carson-Dellosa Publishing Company, Inc.

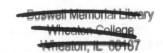

Table of Contents

Table of Contents

Introduction

It is important for students, especially today, to be able to communicate with others. This activity book is designed to help students by focusing on a specific skill: synonyms and antonyms. This will help with the students' knowledge and retention of the skill. Many students do not need all the enrichment activities in the book. The teacher must decide which activities to use to meet the needs of the students. The pages in this book may be used for whole group or individual instruction. Some students may understand the topic after one activity, while others may need more reinforcement.

Teachers are encouraged to copy the pages of this book for use in their classrooms. The exercises will promote the ability to use synonyms and antonyms in writing and speaking.

Synonyms: *Introduction*   SYNONYMS

Synonyms are words that have the same or nearly the same meaning. There are no two words that mean exactly the same thing. Synonyms can have similar meanings when used in some sentences, but they may have different meanings when used in other sentences.

You can usually tell which synonym to use by the context of the sentence.

Jill **hiked** home from school.
Jill **ambled** home from school.
Jill **marched** home from school.

All of the sentences let us know that Jill walked home from school, and so they are synonyms of the word *walk.* The three sentences don't mean the same thing, though. To *hike* is to go on an extended walk with a purpose, to *amble* is to walk in a slow and leisurely manner, to *march* is to walk in a formal manner with measured steps. So even though they all mean "walk," it is necessary to look at the context of the sentence before you choose the correct synonym. Which sentence would you choose if you wanted to say that Jill wasn't in a hurry to get home after school? *Jill ambled home from school* would be the best choice.

If you were writing about a hunter out in search of a deer, which sentence would you pick?

The hunter was **looking for** a deer.
The hunter was **stalking** a deer.
The hunter was **searching for** a deer.

All of the words are synonyms, but *stalking* means to track game, so that is the sentence to choose.

If you were writing about Steven being happy about a good grade in class, which sentence would you choose?

Steven was **glad** when he saw the "A" on his test.
Steven was **gratified** when he saw the "A" on his test.
Steven was **elated** when he saw the "A" on his test.

All of the words are synonyms for *happy,* but *elated* expresses a greater degree of happiness.

When using synonyms, there will be times when you can choose from many synonyms for a word in your sentence. At other times, you will only have one word that can fit exactly.

Name:_____ Date:_____

Synonyms: *Exercise 1*

SYNONYMS

Directions: Find a synonym for each word listed below from among the words in the word bank. Write the synonym on the line.

hat	bright	shore	enemy	stop
talk	quiet	cry	neat	yell
happy	damp	jump	throw	path
little	gazed	home	assist	spin

1. wet _____

2. cap _____

3. house _____

4. shiny _____

5. hop _____

6. small _____

7. shout _____

8. toss _____

9. foe _____

10. halt _____

11. tidy _____

12. glad _____

13. help _____

14. speak _____

15. looked _____

16. trail _____

17. beach _____

18. twirl _____

19. weep _____

20. still _____

Write a paragraph using eight of the synonyms above. Make sure your sentences show that you know the meaning of the words.

_____

_____

_____

_____

_____

_____

Name: _____ Date: _____

Synonyms: *Exercise 2*

SYNONYMS

Directions: In the following exercise, choose the synonym for each of the words. Write your choice on the line.

1.	happy	_____	glad, bad, nervous
2.	guest	_____	helper, visitor, student
3.	complete	_____	begin, finish, start
4.	simple	_____	easy, hard, difficult
5.	twirl	_____	move, spin, walk
6.	fast	_____	walk, quick, slow
7.	walk	_____	go, stroll, speak
8.	comical	_____	unhappy, funny, caring
9.	noisy	_____	smell, soft, loud
10.	yank	_____	pull, carry, wait
11.	trash	_____	books, litter, strange
12.	gone	_____	absent, waiting, neat
13.	donate	_____	ask, give, meet
14.	error	_____	mistake, answer, test
15.	howled	_____	cried, wished, wanted
16.	funny	_____	perfect, silly, careful
17.	fell	_____	toppled, moved, skipped
18.	near	_____	act, plain, close
19.	wealthy	_____	happy, rich, sad
20.	mend	_____	remain, think, repair

Name: _____ Date: _____

Synonyms: *Exercise 3*

SYNONYMS

Directions: In the following exercise, choose the synonym for each of the words. Write your choice on the line.

1.	incinerate	_____	burn, buy, finish
2.	brave	_____	funny, bold, happy
3.	act	_____	involve, perform, persuade
4.	inquire	_____	purchase, inform, ask
5.	carve	_____	draw, cut, stitch
6.	shatter	_____	break, remove, gather
7.	locate	_____	misplace, find, need
8.	shun	_____	stop, think, avoid
9.	alike	_____	different, same, love
10.	sole	_____	fish, shoe, only
11.	accept	_____	receive, renew, repair
12.	clumsy	_____	needy, careful, awkward
13.	border	_____	space, edge, mark
14.	decline	_____	lie, refuse, decide
15.	choose	_____	select, run, escape
16.	dangerous	_____	special, risky, odd
17.	inexpensive	_____	blast, dear, cheap
18.	courteous	_____	adept, polite, bow
19.	pursue	_____	chase, lead, money
20.	command	_____	order, remove, inquire

4

Name: _____ Date: _____

Synonyms: *Exercise 4*

SYNONYMS

Directions: In the following exercise, choose the synonym for each of the words. Write your choice on the line.

1. conquer   _____   defeat, dismiss, care

2. maybe   _____   want, perhaps, wish

3. coarse   _____   smooth, class, rough

4. common   _____   colorful, ordinary, special

5. procrastinate   _____   dawdle, wait, hurry

6. eager   _____   easy, slow, enthusiastic

7. disease   _____   illness, unhappy, health

8. surprise   _____   know, ordinary, amaze

9. happen   _____   occur, skip, wait

10. entry   _____   ticket, beg, door

11. dense   _____   smooth, thick, smart

12. outcome   _____   indoors, flavor, result

13. capture   _____   hat, seize, success

14. tired   _____   weary, attempt, alert

15. empty   _____   full, vacant, important

16. eject   _____   display, discharge, simple

17. purchase   _____   buy, need, sell

18. abode   _____   residence, tree, fearful

19. ask   _____   tell, inquire, listen

20. average   _____   count, normal, special

Name: _____ Date: _____

Synonyms: *Exercise 5*

SYNONYMS

Directions: In the following sentences, write the correct synonym from the word bank in the blank space.

absent	carve	vacant	flavor	gentle
timid	leave	purchase	pick	fib
laughed	ill	ache	trip	awards

1. Tom told a _____ (lie) when he said he wasn't at the ballgame.

2. My family took a _____ (journey) to Florida last summer.

3. Carol was _____ (shy) the first day of school.

4. I have to _____ (go) at 6:00 tonight.

5. On Wednesday, I am going to _____ (buy) a new book at the mall.

6. We are going to _____ (select) our teams in gym today.

7. Beth is _____ (gone) from school this week.

8. On Halloween I get to _____ (cut) the pumpkin.

9. Our school has an assembly to give out the academic _____ (prizes).

10. Our student council is going to clean up the _____ (empty) lot by our school.

11. The _____ (pain) in my mouth is from a cavity.

12. You must be very _____ (kind) to baby animals.

13. This new gum has a cinnamon _____ (taste).

14. We all _____ (giggled) at Bill's funny joke.

15. Liz and Barb are both _____ (sick) with the flu.

Name: _____ Date: _____

Synonyms: *Exercise 6*   SYNONYMS

Directions: In the following sentences, write the correct synonym from the word bank in the blank space.

pause	annoy	hopped	friends	street
scampered	shoved	guests	shattered	beach
quit	gather	cooperate	raise	rush

1. The squirrel _____ (ran) across the yard to the tree.

2. The glass _____ (broke) when it fell off the counter.

3. Jack and Jeff _____ (pushed) the large boat into the water.

4. Carri and Todd made sandcastles on the _____ (shore).

5. Mom is expecting _____ (visitors) this afternoon.

6. Don't _____ (hurry) your science experiment; it might fail.

7. We sometimes _____ (stop) the videotape to have a class discussion.

8. The frog _____ (jumped) into the pond.

9. The bus stop is at the end of our _____ (road).

10. My _____ (pals) and I are going to the movies tonight.

11. Students who talk in class _____ (bother) the teacher.

12. At summer camp, we _____ (lift) the flag every morning.

13. Michael is going to _____ (stop) playing baseball.

14. All team members need to _____ (help) to win the game.

15. We have to _____ (collect) 100 names for our petition.

Name:_____ Date:_____

Synonyms: *Exercise 7*

SYNONYMS

Directions: In the following groups of words, circle the one that is not a synonym for the others.

1.	illness	sickness	disease	health
2.	smile	grin	frown	laugh
3.	crazy	serious	silly	foolish
4.	fellow	woman	lady	female
5.	unhappy	sad	depressed	joyful
6.	excited	calm	quiet	restful
7.	amble	race	walk	stroll
8.	type	draw	sketch	trace
9.	eat	chew	dine	starve
10.	excited	weary	tired	drowsy
11.	happy	thrilled	sad	excited
12.	decrease	inform	lessen	decline
13.	accurate	perfect	inspect	correct
14.	joke	pun	quip	idle
15.	start	mend	repair	fix
16.	hop	jump	tardy	leap
17.	knife	major	lance	sword
18.	yell	scream	talk	shout
19.	swift	stern	fast	rapid
20.	gaze	observe	pitch	look

Name: _____ Date: _____

Synonyms: *Exercise 8*

SYNONYMS

Directions: In the following groups of words, circle the one that is not a synonym for the others.

1.	glance	look	observe	under
2.	foe	antagonist	friend	enemy
3.	mural	make	create	produce
4.	quiet	quickly	peaceful	calm
5.	talk	speak	wilted	inform
6.	darken	dim	shining	shade
7.	river	rushing	stream	creek
8.	fearful	bold	brave	fearless
9.	closed	shut	sled	sealed
10.	few	some	much	several
11.	mountain	pebble	stone	rock
12.	ship	boat	shop	yacht
13.	current	curious	new	modern
14.	vapor	visor	fume	smoke
15.	rip	ripe	tear	split
16.	tip	race	run	dash
17.	gentle	kind	tough	caring
18.	clearly	clothes	apparel	garments
19.	clip	snip	crop	spell
20.	chuckle	chicken	giggle	snicker

Name:_____ Date:_____

Synonyms: *Exercise 9*

SYNONYMS

Directions: Write a synonym for each clue below in the crossword puzzle.

ACROSS	**DOWN**
4. begin	1. error
6. noisy	2. ask
7. same	3. unhappy
9. always	5. pile
10. buy	8. late
14. silly	11. nap
15. wide	12. walk
16. ill	13. throw
17. talk	17. easy
18. assist	
19. middle	

10

Name: _____   Date: _____

Synonyms: *Exercise 10*   SYNONYMS

Directions: Write a synonym for each word. On the line below each word write a sentence using the synonym. Use a dictionary if you need help.

1. A synonym for **author** is _____

_____

2. A synonym for **smell** is _____

_____

3. A synonym for **act** is _____

_____

4. A synonym for **maybe** is _____

_____

5. A synonym for **tough** is _____

_____

6. A synonym for **correct** is _____

_____

7. A synonym for **mist** is _____

_____

8. A synonym for **voyage** is _____

_____

9. A synonym for **basement** is _____

_____

10. A synonym for **dungeon** is _____

_____

Name:_____ Date:_____

Synonyms: *Exercise 11*

SYNONYMS

Directions: Write a synonym for each word. On the line below each word write a sentence using the synonym. Use a dictionary if you need help.

1. A synonym for **affection** is _____

    _____

2. A synonym for **robber** is _____

    _____

3. A synonym for **rock** is _____

    _____

4. A synonym for **risky** is _____

    _____

5. A synonym for **sleep** is _____

    _____

6. A synonym for **splatter** is _____

    _____

7. A synonym for **see** is _____

    _____

8. A synonym for **sour** is _____

    _____

9. A synonym for **listen** is _____

    _____

10. A synonym for **oath** is _____

    _____

Name:_____ Date:_____

Synonyms: *Exercise 12*

SYNONYMS

Directions: Read the following pairs of words. If they are synonyms, write yes; if they are not synonyms, write no. Use a dictionary if you need help.

1.	happy	sad	_____	16. walk	amble	_____
2.	sick	ill	_____	17. throw	catch	_____
3.	create	build	_____	18. eat	chew	_____
4.	weary	tired	_____	19. sleep	nap	_____
5.	rough	flat	_____	20. tiny	large	_____
6.	foggy	misty	_____	21. strike	hit	_____
7.	quick	slow	_____	22. dangerous	risky	_____
8.	delicious	tasty	_____	23. useful	helpful	_____
9.	naughty	nice	_____	24. easy	simple	_____
10.	path	trail	_____	25. flame	fire	_____
11.	perform	act	_____	26. hide	seek	_____
12.	tame	wild	_____	27. little	small	_____
13.	final	last	_____	28. pile	heap	_____
14.	future	past	_____	29. snack	dinner	_____
15.	fake	fraud	_____	30. work	play	_____

Synonyms: *Exercise 13*

SYNONYMS

Name: _____ Date: _____

Directions: Read the following pairs of words. If they are synonyms, write yes; if they are not synonyms, write no. Use a dictionary if you need help.

1.	weak	strong	_____	16.	leave	exit	_____
2.	crawl	creep	_____	17.	muffle	mute	_____
3.	liquid	solid	_____	18.	vanish	disappear	_____
4.	reproduce	copy	_____	19.	damage	repair	_____
5.	oath	vow	_____	20.	fluid	liquid	_____
6.	rabbit	hare	_____	21.	war	peace	_____
7.	loose	tight	_____	22.	rage	anger	_____
8.	illegal	unlawful	_____	23.	shallow	deep	_____
9.	barter	trade	_____	24.	doctor	surgeon	_____
10.	done	finished	_____	25.	ours	theirs	_____
11.	door	entry	_____	26.	vision	sight	_____
12.	grade	rate	_____	27.	nervous	calm	_____
13.	mine	yours	_____	28.	fair	just	_____
14.	begin	start	_____	29.	most	least	_____
15.	lift	raise	_____	30.	same	different	_____

Name:_____ Date:_____

Synonyms: *Exercise 14*   SYNONYMS

Directions: Read the following pairs of words. If they are synonyms, write yes; if they are not synonyms, write no. Use a dictionary if you need help.

1.	bashful	bold	_____	16.	cradle	crib	_____
2.	whiff	scent	_____	17.	dust	lint	_____
3.	remove	eject	_____	18.	take	grab	_____
4.	much	little	_____	19.	feel	touch	_____
5.	moist	damp	_____	20.	useful	useless	_____
6.	entice	lure	_____	21.	ignore	disregard	_____
7.	occupied	busy	_____	22.	innocent	guilty	_____
8.	young	old	_____	23.	smell	fragrance	_____
9.	clench	grip	_____	24.	cool	frosty	_____
10.	tardy	early	_____	25.	borrow	lend	_____
11.	relative	kin	_____	26.	elevate	raise	_____
12.	medal	award	_____	27.	tell	listen	_____
13.	mend	patch	_____	28.	jaunt	trip	_____
14.	hurt	injure	_____	29.	outer	inner	_____
15.	pity	sympathy	_____	30.	irritate	bother	_____

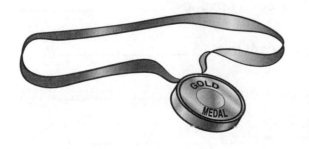

Name: _____ Date: _____

Synonyms: *Exercise 15*

SYNONYMS

Directions: Read each of the following sentences. Choose the correct synonym for the underlined word from the word bank and write it on the line. Use a dictionary if you need help.

ache	mistake	unhappy	idle	connect
below	brook	wealthy	stroll	comical
perhaps	rage	remain	ill	swift

1. My brother was very <u>angry</u>; he was in a _____.

2. When I hit my thumb with the hammer, I felt <u>pain</u>; I felt a terrible _____.

3. My grandma said I was <u>lazy</u>; she said I was _____.

4. Yesterday at school I felt <u>sick</u>; I was _____.

5. Would you <u>stay</u> at my house; would you _____ here?

6. I found an <u>error</u> on the paper; that was the only _____.

7. <u>Maybe</u> we should finish the homework. _____ that is the best thing to do.

8. I like to <u>walk</u> after school. I _____ around the block with Mom.

9. The red book is <u>under</u> the green one; see it _____ the green book?

10. I need to <u>join</u> the links of the chain together. Help me _____ them.

11. There is a little <u>stream</u> in the woods; it's a babbling _____.

12. James runs really <u>fast</u>; I have never seen anyone so _____.

13. When I grow up, I want to be <u>rich</u>; I want to be _____.

14. Carol tells such <u>funny</u> jokes; her jokes are really _____.

15. Ben is feeling very <u>sad</u>; I wish he weren't so _____.

Name: _____ Date: _____

Synonyms: *Exercise 16*

SYNONYMS

Directions: Read each of the following sentences. Choose the correct synonym for the underlined word from the word bank and write it on the line. Use a dictionary if you need help.

admit	repair	just	vanished	piece
sly	pull	same	hare	flavor
entry	finished	vow	complete	cut

1. The detective on the case was very <u>clever</u>; he was _____.

2. My homework has <u>disappeared</u>; it has _____ from my book bag.

3. The criminal will <u>confess</u> to the crime; he finally will _____ he stole the ring.

4. Give the cord a <u>yank</u>; give it a hard _____.

5. I like the <u>taste</u> of the new toothpaste; it has the _____ of chocolate.

6. Mrs. Weed wants us to <u>finish</u> this by noon. She said we need to _____ it.

7. In Scouts you take an <u>oath</u>. It is a _____ to follow the rules.

8. I need to <u>mend</u> my jeans. I think I'll _____ them after school.

9. Who wants to <u>carve</u> the pumpkin? I'll _____ the eyes.

10. You're <u>done</u> with your homework? I am not _____ yet.

11. The magician has a <u>rabbit</u> in his act. He pulled the _____ out of a hat.

12. That judge is <u>fair</u>; she gave a _____ verdict.

13. That <u>door</u> over there is the _____ to the cafeteria.

14. Make sure the pieces of cake are <u>equal</u>; I want the _____ size you have.

15. Share <u>part</u> of the pie with me. Give me a _____.

Name: _____ Date: _____

Synonyms: *Exercise 17*   SYNONYMS

Directions: Read each of the following sentences. Choose the correct synonym for the under-lined word from the word bank and write it on the line. Use a dictionary if you need help.

tired	start	grin	collect	odd
interior	perform	awkward	purchase	huge
brag	smell	build	increase	award

1. Jerry <u>boasted</u> that he got an "A" on the test. I wish he didn't _____ so much.

2. When you <u>begin</u> a math problem you should _____ with reading it carefully.

3. The desert was a <u>vast</u> area of sand and cactus. It was _____.

4. Do you recognize that <u>odor</u>? What is that _____?

5. Mom is painting the <u>inside</u> of the house. I think the _____ walls will be yellow.

6. At the farm I <u>gather</u> the eggs; sometimes the chickens won't let me _____ them.

7. I bought a new model to <u>make</u>; I am going to _____ it this afternoon.

8. Student Council needs to <u>buy</u> balloons for the dance. Who will make the _____?

9. Let's <u>add</u> two inches to the circumference; that will _____ the size of the circle.

10. The baby tried to imitate her mother's <u>smile</u> with a silly _____.

11. Did you get first <u>prize</u> in the bake-off? Who did get the _____?

12. I get to <u>act</u> in the play. I _____ the part of the old woman.

13. That worm looks <u>strange</u>. Do you think it looks _____?

14. Jim always looks <u>clumsy</u> on the dance floor; I hope I don't look that _____.

15. Kim feels <u>weary</u> after mowing the grass. She is so _____ that she is going to rest.

18

Name: _____   Date: _____

Synonyms: *Exercise 18*

SYNONYMS

Directions: Write the correct synonym for the word in parentheses from the word bank in the blank. Use a dictionary if you need help.

tidy	vacant	equal	tasks	assist
odor	vanished	decline	consent	wound
explosion	litter	noisy	error	tart

1. Beth and I are _____ (same) in height.

2. Did Dad give you any _____ (jobs) to do after school?

3. What is that strange _____ (smell) coming from your room?

4. Did you have the nurse look at your _____ (injury)?

5. I heard a huge _____ (blast) coming from Main Street.

6. Let's clean up that _____ (empty) lot and plant vegetables.

7. Did you _____ (refuse) Todd's invitation for Saturday?

8. Look at all the _____ (trash) that's been thrown on the field.

9. I think Mom's lemon pie is a little too _____ (sour) for me.

10. Do you need Bill to _____ (help) you with your homework?

11. The concert was very _____ (loud).

12. You need to be very careful; you don't want to make an _____ (mistake).

13. Did your dad _____ (agree) to drive us to the movie theater?

14. The chocolate cake just _____ (disappeared).

15. Debbie, I never realized you were so _____ (neat).

Name: _____ Date: _____

Synonyms: *Exercise 19*

SYNONYMS

Directions: Write the correct synonym for the word in parentheses from the word bank in the blank. Use a dictionary if you need help.

forever	fiesta	parfait	desired
stolen	chat	substitute	succeeded
dampen	synthetic	affectionate	trustworthy
ethical	mysterious	zero	

1. Laura is going to have a _____ (ice cream) for dessert.

2. Can you stay after school and _____ (talk) with me?

3. Linda had her purse _____ (taken) from her locker.

4. My boots are made of _____ (artificial) material.

5. My grandmother is very _____ (loving).

6. In Mexico they have a _____ (festival) on May 5.

7. The coach had to _____ (replace) the pitcher in the fifth inning.

8. Beth is a very _____ (dependable) friend.

9. Before steam irons, you had to _____ (moisten) your clothes and then iron.

10. Cheating on a test is not _____ (moral).

11. The orchestra _____ (followed) the choir in the concert.

12. Annie really _____ (wanted) a kitten.

13. Chuck got a _____ (nothing) on his test.

14. Who is that _____ (strange) person in the book?

15. Peter Pan wanted to be a boy _____ (always).

Name: _____ Date: _____

Synonyms: *Exercise 20*

SYNONYMS

Directions: Write a synonym for each clue below in the crossword puzzle.

	ACROSS		DOWN
5.	accept	1.	response
6.	edit	2.	act
8.	ache	3.	maybe
10.	grime	4.	author
11.	back	5.	refuse
13.	tread	7.	oath
14.	piece	9.	cloudy
15.	tough	10.	jail
16.	spoil	12.	stroll
17.	mild	13.	smell

Name: _____ Date: _____

Synonyms: *Exercise 21*   SYNONYMS

Directions: In the blank following the sentence, write a synonym for the underlined word. Use a dictionary if you need help.

1. We are going to have a <u>test</u> in math today. _____

2. Henry <u>tossed</u> the ball over the volleyball net. _____

3. Todd <u>closed</u> the door with a bang. _____

4. Mike <u>tore</u> his jacket at school. _____

5. Vanessa <u>looked</u> out the window at the snowstorm. _____

6. The relay teams <u>raced</u> to the end of the field. _____

7. Chris threw a <u>rock</u> across the lake. _____

8. Luis was <u>unhappy</u> that he didn't win the election. _____

9. The new <u>cars</u> are being displayed at the fairgrounds. _____

10. It was so hot I came in and <u>swallowed</u> a whole glass of water. _____

11. The racer ran <u>swiftly</u> around the track. _____

12. Liz and Bill had <u>some</u> friends over to their house. _____

13. Did the apples <u>drop</u> from that tree? _____

14. I went to the dentist because I had a <u>pain</u> in my tooth. _____

15. The gym teacher <u>yelled</u> to stop the game. _____

Name: _____ Date: _____

Synonyms: *Exercise 22*

SYNONYMS

Directions: In the blank following the sentence, write a synonym for the underlined word. Use a dictionary if you need help.

1. I was <u>late</u> for school yesterday. _____

2. John must be unhappy; he has a <u>frown</u> on his face today. _____

3. Whose job is it to tell the teacher when our project is <u>finished</u>? _____

4. The picture on the wall looks like it is <u>tilted</u> to the left. _____

5. At Halloween sometimes people play <u>pranks</u> on their neighbors. _____

6. You need to <u>expand</u> these balloons so we can decorate for the party. _____

7. That certainly is an <u>odd</u>-looking rock you brought to class today. _____

8. Whew! That cleaner has a <u>powerful</u> scent. _____

9. Crossing the street without looking is certainly an <u>unwise</u> thing to do. _____

10. My sister always <u>weeps</u> at sad movies. _____

11. Did your mom <u>consent</u> to letting you go to the movie? _____

12. I love to <u>touch</u> the soft fur on kittens. _____

13. When Taylor grows up, she wants to be a famous <u>writer</u>. _____

14. Jordan, did you have your <u>wound</u> looked at by the nurse? _____

15. At Christmas all the shoppers seem to be in a <u>rush</u>. _____

Name:_____ Date:_____

Synonyms: *Exercise 23*

SYNONYMS

Directions: Write a synonym for each clue below in the crossword puzzle.

	ACROSS		DOWN
2.	fact	1.	scared
3.	pledge	4.	inside
5.	tilt	8.	receive
6.	big	9.	unfriendly
7.	about	10.	abroad
10.	hinder	12.	blowup
11.	crawl	13.	loyal
13.	moist	15.	pest
14.	debris	16.	odd
18.	reporter	17.	guard

Name: _____ Date: _____

Synonyms: *Exercise 24*   SYNONYMS

Directions: In each of the following sentences, choose the letter of the synonym of the under-lined word and write the letter on the blank.

_____ 1. I <u>barely</u> made it to class before the bell rang this morning.
    (a) hardly   (b) never   (c) sometimes

_____ 2. Who <u>understands</u> how to do the experiment?
    (a) listens   (b) answers   (c) knows

_____ 3. Would you <u>tell</u> the bus driver where you want to get off?
    (a) inform   (b) question   (c) ask

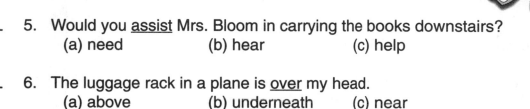

_____ 4. Tim needs to <u>gather</u> butterflies for his group project.
    (a) arrange   (b) collect   (c) throw

_____ 5. Would you <u>assist</u> Mrs. Bloom in carrying the books downstairs?
    (a) need   (b) hear   (c) help

_____ 6. The luggage rack in a plane is <u>over</u> my head.
    (a) above   (b) underneath   (c) near

_____ 7. In England, prisoners were kept in castle <u>dungeons</u>.
    (a) towers   (b) jails   (c) fields

_____ 8. Please divide the candy bar through the <u>center</u>.
    (a) wrapper   (b) edge   (c) middle

_____ 9. After working on the car, it is hard to get the <u>grime</u> off your hands.
    (a) dirt   (b) grease   (c) soap

_____ 10. The soap in the commercial is supposed to be <u>gentle</u> on your skin.
    (a) clean   (b) mild   (c) rough

_____ 11. In Seattle, there are many days that are <u>overcast</u>.
    (a) cloudy   (b) dark   (c) windy

_____ 12. After writing the first draft of your paper, you need to <u>revise</u>.
    (a) repeat   (b) edit   (c) error

_____ 13. Who <u>inquired</u> about the baseball schedule?
    (a) asked   (b) wrote   (c) needed

Name: _____ Date: _____

Synonyms: *Exercise 25*

SYNONYMS

Directions: In each of the following sentences, choose the letter of the synonym of the underlined word and write the letter on the blank.

_____ 1. Who left all the <u>debris</u> on the classroom floor?
(a) rubbish (b) debate (c) cleaning

_____ 2. Next year Lewis is going to study <u>abroad</u>.
(a) home (b) overseas (c) science

_____ 3. Do you <u>promise</u> to meet me at the movies on Friday?
(a) wish (b) want (c) pledge

_____ 4. The road construction will <u>hinder</u> rush-hour traffic.
(a) hide (b) help (c) obstruct

_____ 5. Look at the baby <u>crawl</u> across the floor to her toy.
(a) creep (b) run (c) roll

_____ 6. You need to <u>guard</u> the goal in soccer.
(a) wait (b) watch (c) gaze

_____ 7. Police officers take an <u>oath</u> to protect the citizens.
(a) vow (b) wish (c) note

_____ 8. Ben is <u>loyal</u> to the St. Louis Cardinals baseball team.
(a) helpful (b) devoted (c) excited

_____ 9. That spray will get rid of garden <u>pests</u>.
(a) flowers (b) bugs (c) sticks

_____ 10. You need to <u>tilt</u> the game upward to get the little balls in the holes.
(a) slide (b) turn (c) slant

_____ 11. A snarling dog will <u>frighten</u> me.
(a) scare (b) chase (c) watch

_____ 12. <u>Tread</u> carefully on the new gym floor.
(a) skip (b) look (c) step

_____ 13. What was your <u>response</u> to the teacher?
(a) answer (b) question (c) joke

Road Construction

Name: _____ Date: _____

Synonyms: *Exercise 26*   SYNONYMS

Directions: In each of the following sentences, choose the letter of the synonym of the under-lined word and write the letter on the blank.

_____ 1. We needed to use <u>coarse</u> sandpaper on our wooden bookshelves.
   (a) rough   (b) new   (c) smooth

_____ 2. It is always a good idea to warm up before exercising to <u>stretch</u> your muscles.
   (a) move   (b) lengthen   (c) shorten

_____ 3. Do you <u>recall</u> how to make chocolate chip cookies?
   (a) remember   (b) revise   (c) forget

_____ 4. No one can put a <u>value</u> on a good education.
   (a) sight   (b) worth   (c) stamp

_____ 5. Will you help me <u>locate</u> my glasses?
   (a) lose   (b) check   (c) find

_____ 6. Jeff is going to <u>arrange</u> the chairs for the meeting.
   (a) group   (b) move   (c) scatter

_____ 7. Karen was the <u>sole</u> winner of the spelling bee.
   (a) fish   (b) only   (c) first

_____ 8. Our principal will <u>accept</u> the award for the whole school.
   (a) read   (b) give   (c) receive

_____ 9. Caroline was <u>tardy</u> to class three times last week.
   (a) late   (b) first   (c) running

_____ 10. Are you going to <u>remain</u> after school for football practice?
   (a) leave   (b) stay   (c) look

_____ 11. The pirate ship <u>captured</u> the merchant ship in the old movie.
   (a) seized   (b) sank   (c) painted

_____ 12. My uncle likes to <u>pitch</u> horseshoes.
   (a) nail   (b) toss   (c) catch

_____ 13. Our cat, Tigger, is sometimes <u>hostile</u> to our dog, Rusty.
   (a) happy   (b) unfriendly   (c) friendly

Name:_____ Date:_____

Synonyms: *Exercise 27*

SYNONYMS

Directions: Read the sentences below. Choose your own synonym for the word in parentheses to go in the blank. Make sure that you can justify it. Use a dictionary to help you.

1. During the rainstorm, I was _____ (scared).

2. William has six _____ (mistakes) on his paper.

3. Be _____ (careful) when working with power tools.

4. Don't _____ (ruin) the tower that you just built.

5. How do you think we should _____ (group) the chairs?

6. The plate _____ (broke) when it hit the floor.

7. Mrs. Forest needs to _____ (delay) the beginning of the field trip.

8. What do you think they are going to _____ (build) on that lot?

9. That was really a _____ (funny) story we just read.

10. Let's call some _____ (friends) and see if they want to go to a movie.

11. The police _____ (chased) the robber through the alleys.

12. I have to _____ (agree) that you were right about the score.

13. When do you think that will ever _____ (happen)?

14. Dad likes to come home and _____ (sleep) on the couch.

15. After baseball practice, I am so _____ (tired).

Name:_____ Date:_____

Synonyms: *Exercise 28*

SYNONYMS

Directions: Complete the following story with a synonym for each word in parentheses. Use a dictionary if necessary.

I have a very (big) _____ cat. I have had him for eight years. Some days

I am (happy) _____ to see him, and some days I am not. He isn't very (neat)

_____, and he (throws) _____ his cat food out of his dish. Then

I am (unhappy) _____ with him. Other times he greets me and wants me to pet

him. I like the (touch) _____ of his fur. Because he is so big, he is never in a

(hurry) _____ to get anywhere. I think that if a mouse came into our house,

Tigger would just (lift) _____ his head and (look) _____ at it.

His size may make the mouse (exit) _____. Tigger likes the (interior)

_____ of the house better than the (exterior) _____, especially

in the summer. He doesn't like to get too (warm) _____. Even though he is a

(foolish) _____ cat and he is (idle) _____ and doesn't like (odd)

_____ or (noisy) _____ noises, I think I will keep him. He is

(kind) _____ and we (love) _____ him.

Synonyms: *Synonyms That Can't Be Substituted for Each Other*

SYNONYMS

Some words are synonyms, but because of the context of the sentence, they can't be substituted for each other.

Examples:

Twitch and *jerk* are synonyms for each other because they have the same basic meaning, "to move suddenly."

Look at these sentences:

The rabbit sat quietly except for a twitch of its nose.
or
The rabbit sat quietly except for a jerk of its nose.

Jerk doesn't sound right in the sentence because a jerk is a different kind of movement than a twitch.

Frown and *scowl* are synonyms for each other because they have the same basic meaning, "to lower or contract the brow."

Look at these sentences:

The angry shopkeeper scowled at the boys who broke his window.
or
The angry shopkeeper frowned at the boys who broke his window.

Frowned doesn't sound right in the sentence because a scowl is more intense than a frown.

So when you choose a synonym for your sentence, make sure that you have the one that best fits the context and meaning of the sentence.

Name: _____ Date: _____

Synonyms: *Exercise 29*

SYNONYMS

Directions: In the following sentences, choose the best synonym for the sentence. Circle the correct answer.

1. My brother and my dad hunt in the fall (looking for, stalking) deer.

2. We were (floating, sailing) down the river on our inner tubes.

3. I was so (excited, nervous) about going to Disney World that I couldn't eat breakfast.

4. Could I have a (part, piece) of the cherry pie?

5. Amanda needed a (plain, simple) sheet of paper to draw the picture.

6. The criminal was sentenced to ten years of hard (work, labor).

7. At Halloween I like to (carve, cut) the pumpkin.

8. People on the Oregon Trail had a long (journey, trip) before them.

9. The (strange, mysterious) man worked for the CIA.

10. My sister (collects, gathers) autographs of famous people.

11. Bob needs to (mend, repair) the broken spoke on his bicycle.

12. Andrew has been (late, tardy) to class several times this year.

13. Carri (frowned, scowled) when she didn't understand the question.

14. The rain (toppled, fell) on the roof.

15. We need to (inflate, expand) one hundred balloons for the party.

Synonyms: *Synonyms in the Dictionary* SYNONYMS

Dictionaries often include synonyms after the definition of the word. The abbreviation for synonym, syn., is sometimes at the beginning of the list. All dictionaries do not have synonyms for the words.

Example:

moment n. - Syn. minute, instant, trice, wink, second, jiffy, flash.

These are all synonyms for *moment*, but they do not all have the same meaning. You must be careful when you are choosing a synonym.

Name:_____ Date:_____

Synonyms: *Exercise 30*

SYNONYMS

Directions: Look up the following words in the dictionary. Write two synonyms for each of the words. Then write a sentence for each of the synonyms. Try switching the synonyms in your sentences. Do they still make sense?

	Synonym	**Synonym**

1. heavy _____   _____

    a. _____

    b. _____

2. intelligent _____   _____

    a. _____

    b. _____

3. clever _____   _____

    a. _____

    b. _____

4. error _____   _____

    a. _____

    b. _____

5. throw _____   _____

    a. _____

    b. _____

6. ask _____   _____

    a. _____

    b. _____

Name:_____ Date:_____

Synonyms: *Exercise 31*

SYNONYMS

Directions: Look up the following words in the dictionary. Write two synonyms for each of the words. Then write a sentence for each of the synonyms. Try switching the synonyms in your sentences. Do they still make sense?

	Synonym	**Synonym**
1. cry	_____	_____

a. _____

b. _____

2. begin	_____	_____

a. _____

b. _____

3. smile	_____	_____

a. _____

b. _____

4. bright	_____	_____

a. _____

b. _____

5. stay	_____	_____

a. _____

b. _____

6. shake	_____	_____

a. _____

b. _____

Synonyms: *Synonyms in a Thesaurus* SYNONYMS

There are two types of thesauruses. One is set up just like a dictionary. If you need to know the synonym of a word, you look the word up just as you would in the dictionary, and the synonyms are listed after the word. A more traditional thesaurus has the words listed in the back of the book in an index, and there are guide numbers to direct you to the word you are looking for and the synonyms.

Example: Look up the word *hope* in the index in the back of the thesaurus. The guide number is 858. Then, in the body of the book, go to 858 and you will find the synonyms for the word *hope*.

Name: _____ Date: _____

Synonyms: *Exercise 32*

SYNONYMS

Directions: Using a traditional thesaurus, look up the following words in the index and write the guide numbers on the lines following the words. Then write one of the synonyms listed for each word.

	Guide Number	**Synonym**
1. pain	_____	_____
2. discourtesy	_____	_____
3. boat	_____	_____
4. raft	_____	_____
5. age	_____	_____
6. jury	_____	_____
7. traveler	_____	_____
8. cheap	_____	_____
9. fear	_____	_____
10. murder	_____	_____
11. spite	_____	_____
12. sunset	_____	_____
13. focus	_____	_____
14. passenger	_____	_____
15. herb	_____	_____
16. space	_____	_____
17. repeat	_____	_____
18. bucket	_____	_____
19. gravel	_____	_____
20. handsome	_____	_____

Synonyms: *Exercise 33*

SYNONYMS

Name:_____ Date:_____

Directions: Using a traditional thesaurus, look up the following words in the index and write the guide numbers on the lines following the words. Then write one of the synonyms listed for each word.

		Guide Number	**Synonym**
1.	density	_____	_____
2.	price (money)	_____	_____
3.	ship (vessel)	_____	_____
4.	answer (inquiry)	_____	_____
5.	limit (boundary)	_____	_____
6.	speech	_____	_____
7.	writing	_____	_____
8.	belief	_____	_____
9.	habit (custom)	_____	_____
10.	school (academy)	_____	_____

Directions: Using your thesaurus, answer the following questions.

11. What word has the guide number 1? _____

12. What word has the guide number 656? _____

13. What word has the guide number 378? _____

14. What word has the guide number 1000? _____

15. What word has the guide number 500? _____

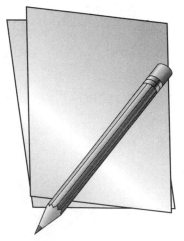

Name:_____ Date:_____

Synonyms: *Exercise 34*

SYNONYMS

Directions: A word can have several synonyms. Write the word on the blank that is not a synonym for the other words.

1. old   elderly   young   antique   aged   _____

2. intelligent smart   forgetful   clever   brainy   _____

3. friend   pal   enemy   companion   chum   _____

4. dread   happy   fear   horror   alarm   _____

5. cry   weep   laugh   sob   wail   _____

6. chuckle   laugh   snicker   moan   giggle   _____

7. purpose   perhaps   aim   goal   mission   _____

8. adorn   simplify   decorate   ornament   beautify   _____

9. wither   fail   thrive   decline   shrivel   _____

10. certain   definite   dubious   sure   positive   _____

11. open   secretive   private   clandestine hidden   _____

12. screen   hide   conceal   cover   view   _____

13. kind   brutal   considerate tender   pleasant   _____

14. finished   done   continuing   through   fulfilled   _____

15. mend   repair   fix   rip   patch   _____

Name:_____ Date:_____

Synonyms: *Exercise 35*

SYNONYMS

Directions: A word can have several synonyms. Write the word on the blank that is not a synonym for the other words.

1. judge   evaluate   appraise   appease   assess   _____

2. thin   slender   robust   slim   narrow   _____

3. wicked   corrupt   honest   evil   immoral   _____

4. formed   shaped   molded   shapeless   fixed   _____

5. logical   senseless   illogical   silly   foolish   _____

6. stop   stir   instigate   urge   plead   _____

7. lessen   decrease   depreciate   diminish   expand   _____

8. cautious   imprudent   discreet   careful   heedful   _____

9. push   shove   crowd   yank   crush   _____

10. spotless   clean   dirty   chaste   washed   _____

11. locate   discover   lose   find   determine   _____

12. enlarge   expand   spread   swell   deflate   _____

13. job   task   vocation   play   career   _____

14. turbulent   violent   calm   noisy   stormy   _____

15. flavor   tang   taste   truant   savor   _____

Name: _____ Date: _____

Synonyms: *Exercise 36*

SYNONYMS

Directions: A word can have several synonyms. Write the word on the blank that is not a synonym for the other words.

1.	rain	sprinkle	drizzle	vapor	shower
2.	create	form	destroy	build	erect
3.	expulsion	removal	remain	purge	suspension
4.	abandon	continue	quit	leave	discontinue
5.	good	respectable	evil	honest	just
6.	crowd	isolate	confine	detach	seclude
7.	education	training	failure	schooling	instruction
8.	empty	hollow	occupied	vacant	blank
9.	regular	uneven	equal	like	same
10.	keep	hold	retain	release	grip
11.	jump	skip	wait	bound	hurdle
12.	confused	bewildered	muddled	advanced	puzzled
13.	active	tired	exhausted	fatigued	wasted
14.	kick	jolt	deprive	jar	hit
15.	almost	nearly	entire	roughly	most

Name:_____ Date:_____

Synonyms: *Exercise 37*

SYNONYMS

Directions: Some words have more than one synonym. Choose from the word bank the synonyms for the words below. Write the synonyms on the lines below each word.

daring	debate	terror	anxious	downy	frightened	pal
nervous	fearless	smooth	valiant	assemble	round	shout
bellow	twist	fright	comrade	anxiety	explain	unite
cry	dispute	shriek	deform	associate	buckle	fearful
playmate	heroic	chum	argue	silky	dread	delicate
convene

discuss

_____

_____

_____

_____

afraid

_____

_____

_____

_____

brave

_____

_____

_____

_____

yell

_____

_____

_____

_____

bend

_____

_____

_____

_____

friend

_____

_____

_____

_____

soft

_____

_____

_____

_____

meet

_____

_____

_____

_____

fear

_____

_____

_____

_____

Name:_____ Date:_____

Synonyms: *Exercise 38*

SYNONYMS

Directions: Some words have more than one synonym. Choose from the word bank the synonyms for the words below. Write the synonyms on the lines below each word.

booming	garbage	ill	unite	totally	soaked	deafening
moist	sodden	acquire	resonant	gloat	bluster	capture
brag	join	diseased	wholly	grab	seize	procure
purchase	noise	snatch	infirm	redeem	invalid	waste
litter	combine	single	damp	refuse	unique	attach
flaunt						

loud

_____

_____

_____

_____

connect

_____

_____

_____

_____

wet

_____

_____

_____

_____

trash

_____

_____

_____

_____

only

_____

_____

_____

_____

buy

_____

_____

_____

_____

sick

_____

_____

_____

_____

boast

_____

_____

_____

_____

catch

_____

_____

_____

_____

Synonyms: *Exercise 39*

SYNONYMS

Directions: Some words have more than one synonym. Choose from the word bank the synonyms for the words below. Write the synonyms on the lines below each word.

stringent	stern	vend	lovely	significant	jubilee	irregularly
festival	essential	hardly	level	joyfully	chill	even
frigid	merrily	attractive	auction	nippy	beautiful	frosty
principal	market	severe	seldom	great	exchange	laughingly
austere	cute	holiday	gladly	horizontal	smooth	anniversary
infrequently						

celebration

_____

_____

_____

_____

sell

_____

_____

_____

_____

important

_____

_____

_____

_____

pretty

_____

_____

_____

_____

occasionally

_____

_____

_____

_____

strict

_____

_____

_____

_____

happily

_____

_____

_____

_____

flat

_____

_____

_____

_____

cool

_____

_____

_____

_____

Synonyms: *Synonym List*

SYNONYMS

abandon - leave

abode - residence

about - nearly

abroad - overseas

absent - gone

accept - receive

accurate - correct

accurate - perfect

ache - pain

ache - throb

acrobat - gymnast

acquire - buy

act - perform

add - increase

admit - confess

adorn - decorate

afraid - nervous

agree - consent

aim - goal

alike - same

allow - grant

almost - nearly

almost - roughly

always - forever

amble - walk

anniversary - celebration

annoy - bother

answer - response

apparel - garments

appraise - assess

arrange - group

artificial - synthetic

ask - inquire

assist - help

author - writer

average - normal

award - prize

back - rear

barely - hardly

barter - trade

beach - shore

below - under

bend - buckle

bend - deform

bend - round

big - huge

blast - explosion

blend - mix

blowup - explosion

boast - bluster

boast - brag

boast - flaunt

boast - gloat

boat - yacht

bold - fearless

booming - loud

border - edge

bound - hurdle

brave - bold

brave - valiant

bravery - courage

bright - shiny

brook - stream

bug - pest

build - erect

buy - procure

buy - purchase

buy - redeem

calm - quiet

calm - restful

capture - seize

carve - cut

catch - capture

catch - grab

catch - seize

catch - snatch

cautious - careful

celebration - festival

celebration - holiday

center - middle

certain - definite

choose - select

chuckle - giggle

chuckle - laugh

chum - friend

clandestine - secret

clench - grip

clever - brainy

clip - snip

closed - shut

clothes - apparel

clothes - garments

cloudy - overcast

clumsy - awkward

coarse - rough

combine - connect

comical - funny

command - order

common - ordinary

44

Synonyms: *Synonym List*

SYNONYMS

companion - chum
complete - finish
conceal - cover
confused - bewildered
connect - join
connect - unite
conquer - defeat
considerate - pleasant
cool - chill
cool - frigid
cool - frosty
cool - nippy
cooperate - help
courteous - polite
cradle - crib
crawl - creep
crazy - silly
create - build
create - form
create - produce
crowd - crush
cry - weep
current - new
cut - carve
damp - wet
dangerous - risky
darken - dim
debris - rubbish
declare - state
decline - decrease
decline - refuse
decorate - ornament
decrease - lessen

definite - sure
delicious - tasty
dense - thick
dependable - trustworthy
depreciate - diminish
devoted - loyal
dim - shade
disappeared - vanished
discontinue - quit
discover - determine
discreet - cautious
discuss - debate
discuss - dispute
discuss - argue
discuss - explain
disease - illness
diseased - ill
doctor - surgeon
donate - give
done - finished
done - through
door - entry
draw - sketch
dread - fear
drizzle - shower
dungeons - jails
dust - lint
eager - enthusiastic
easy - simple
eat - chew
eat - dine
edit - revise
educated - trained

eject - discharge
elderly - aged
elevate - raise
empty - hollow
empty - vacant
enemy - antagonist
enemy - foe
enlarge - expand
entice - lure
entry - door
equal - same
error - mistake
even - flat
evil - immoral
excited - nervous
exhausted - tired
expand - swell
expensive - costly
expensive - dear
expulsion - removal
fact - truth
fail - decline
fair - just
fake - fraud
fast - quick
fast - rapid
fear - alarm
fear - dread
fear - horror
fear - terror
feel - touch
fell - toppled
female - woman

45

Synonyms: *Synonym List*

SYNONYMS

festival - fiesta	grade - rate	important - essential
few - some	grime - dirt	important - great
fib - lie	grin - smile	important - principal
final - last	guard - watch	important - significant
finished - done	guest - visitor	incinerate - burn
flame - fire	happen - occur	inexpensive - cheap
flat - even	happily - gladly	infirm - sick
flat - horizontal	happily - joyfully	inflate - expand
flat - level	happily - laughingly	injury - wound
flavor - taste	happily - merrily	inquire - ask
floating - sailing	happy - glad	inside - interior
fluid - liquid	happy - joyful	instigate - urge
foe - enemy	happy - thrilled	intelligent - smart
foggy - misty	hare - rabbit	irregularly - occasionally
followed - succeeded	heap - pile	irritate - bother
formed - shaped	help - assist	isolate - seclude
friend - comrade	hidden - private	jail - dungeon
friend - pal	hide - conceal	jaunt - trip
friends - pals	hinder - obstruct	job - task
frighten - scare	home - house	joke - pun
frightened - afraid	honest - respectable	joke - quip
frown - scowl	hop - jump	journey - trip
funny - silly	hop - leap	jubilee - celebration
gather - collect	hostile - unfriendly	judge - evaluate
gaze - observe	howled - cried	jump - hop
gazed - looked	hurt - injure	just - fair
gentle - caring	ice cream - parfait	keep - retain
gentle - kind	idle - lazy	kick - jolt
gentle - mild	ignore - disregard	kind - considerate
giggle - snicker	ill - sick	knife - sword
gladly - happily	illegal - unlawful	late - tardy
glance - look	illness - sickness	laugh - snicker
gone - absent	illogical - senseless	laugh - giggle

46

Synonyms: *Synonym List*

SYNONYMS

leave - exit	neat - tidy	pity - sympathy
leave - go	new - modern	plain - simple
lessen - decrease	noisy - loud	pledge - promise
level - flat	nothing - zero	pretty - attractive
lift - raise	oath - vow	pretty - beautiful
litter - trash	occasionally - hardly	pretty - cute
little - small	occasionally - infrequently	pretty - lovely
locate - find	occasionally - seldom	private - secretive
look - observe	occupied - busy	prize - award
loud - deafening	odd - strange	procrastinate - dawdle
loud - noisy	odor - smell	promise - pledge
loving - affectionate	old - antique	purchase - buy
loyal - devoted	old - elderly	pull - yank
mad - angry	only - single	purpose - aim
make - build	only - sole	purpose - mission
make - create	only - totally	pursue - chase
maybe - perhaps	only - unique	push - shove
medal - award	only - wholly	quiet - calm
meet - assemble	ornament - beautify	quiet - peaceful
meet - associate	outcome - result	quiet - still
meet - convene	over - above	quit - stop
mend - repair	overcast - cloudy	rabbit - hare
mend - fix	part - piece	race - run
middle - center	path - trail	rage - anger
mild - gentle	pause - stop	rain - sprinkle
mistake - error	pebble - stone	raise - lift
moist - damp	perform - act	real - genuine
moisten - dampen	perhaps - maybe	recall - remember
molded - shaped	pest - bug	receive - accept
moral - ethical	pick - select	refuse - decline
muffle - mute	piece - part	refuse - reject
nap - rest	pile - heap	refuse - trash
near - close	pitch - toss	relative - kin

Synonyms: *Synonym List*

SYNONYMS

remain - stay	silky - soft	stream - brook
removal - purge	silly - foolish	stream - creek
remove - eject	simple - easy	street - road
repair - fix	slant - tilt	stretch - lengthen
repair - mend	sleep - nap	strict - austere
repeat - recite	slim - narrow	strict - stern
replace - substitute	sly - clever	strict - stringent
reporter - newspaperman	smart - clever	strike - hit
reproduce - copy	smell - fragrance	stroll - walk
response - answer	smell - odor	sure - positive
revise - edit	smell - scent	surprise - amaze
rich - wealthy	smile - grin	swift - fast
rip - tear	smile - laugh	sword - lance
river - stream	smoke - fume	table - graph
rubbish - debris	snip - crop	take - grab
run - dash	sob - wail	taken - stolen
rush - hurry	soft - downy	talk - chat
sad - depressed	soft - delicate	talk - inform
same - alike	soft - smooth	talk - speak
same - equal	soft - silky	tardy - late
scampered - ran	sole - only	taste - flavor
scared - frightened	some - several	tasty - delicious
scream - shout	sour - tart	tell - inform
screen - hide	speak - utter	thin - slender
sell - auction	spin - twirl	thrilled - excited
shatter - break	spoil - decay	throw - toss
shattered - broke	stay - remain	tidy - neat
ship - boat	step - tread	tilt - slant
shove - push	stone - pebble	timid - shy
shun - avoid	stone - rock	tired - drowsy
shut - sealed	stop - halt	tired - weary
sick - ill	strange - mysterious	toppled - fell
sick - invalid	strange - odd	torn - split

Synonyms: *Synonym List*

SYNONYMS

toss - throw

tough - strong

trash - garbage

trash - litter

trash - refuse

trash - waste

tread - step

trip - journey

twirl - spin

understands - knows

unfriendly - hostile

unhappy - sad

untrue - false

useful - helpful

vacant - empty

value - worth

vanish - disappear

vanished - disappeared

vapor - smoke

vast - huge

vision - sight

vocation - career

vow - oath

wait - delay

walk - amble

walk - stroll

wanted - desired

wealthy - rich

weary - tired

weep - sob

wet - damp

wet - moist

wet - sodden

whiff - scent

wicked - corrupt

wide - broad

wither - shrivel

woman - lady

work - labor

yank - pull

yell - bellow

yell - scream

yell - shout

yell - shriek

Antonyms: *Introduction*

ANTONYMS

An **antonym** of a word is a word with the opposite meaning. There usually aren't as many choices for antonyms for a word as there are synonyms. It is important to choose the best antonym for your sentence.

Examples: *Hot* is an antonym of *cold.*

Warm is an antonym of *cold.*

When choosing the antonym, you must think about the context of your sentence. Did your glass of water sit on the counter for an hour and become warm rather than cold, or were you standing outside in 90 degree weather and became hot rather than cold?

Examples: *Soft* is an antonym of *hard.*

Easy is an antonym of *hard.*

In this example, you must know if your sentence is about some surface that is hard or soft or if it is about a task that is easy or hard.

Some antonyms are formed by adding a prefix that means "not."

Examples: *Unhappy* is an antonym of *happy.*

Unavailable is an antonym of *available.*

Nonfiction is an antonym of *fiction.*

Nonflammable is an antonym of *flammable.*

Disappear is an antonym of *appear.*

Dislike is an antonym of *like.*

A dictionary sometimes lists antonyms at the end of an entry for a word. Antonyms come after the synonyms. A thesaurus also will list antonyms after the synonyms for a word.

Antonyms: *Exercise 1*

Name:_____ Date:_____

ANTONYMS

Directions: Find the correct antonym in the word bank for each word below and write it on the line.

fiction	rested	messy	front	over
rough	narrow	end	full	sad
ask	shiny	quiet	early	last
cruel	short	well	sell	go

1. smooth _____

2. neat _____

3. tell _____

4. first _____

5. under _____

6. sick _____

7. fact _____

8. wide _____

9. kind _____

10. begin _____

11. back _____

12. tired _____

13. buy _____

14. happy _____

15. dull _____

16. late _____

17. tall _____

18. empty _____

19. noisy _____

20. stay _____

Write a paragraph using eight of the antonyms above. Make sure that your sentences show that you know the meaning of the words.

_____

_____

_____

_____

_____

_____

Name: _____ Date: _____

Antonyms: *Exercise 2*

ANTONYMS

Directions: In the following exercise, choose the antonym for each of the words. Write your choice on the line.

1. some   _____   none, all, many

2. tender   _____   loving, tough, special

3. discard   _____   disappear, throw, keep

4. visible   _____   slight, invisible, inside

5. scream   _____   whisper, yell, talk

6. mine   _____   yours, you, me

7. hide   _____   disappear, seek, tan

8. attack   _____   defend, attach, fight

9. early   _____   morning, late, ahead

10. deep   _____   thick, dense, shallow

11. often   _____   many, seldom, always

12. limp   _____   soft, stagger, stiff

13. achieve   _____   fail, accept, invent

14. last   _____   final, first, fine

15. specific   _____   exact, even, vague

16. cage   _____   trap, release, pen

17. normal   _____   unusual, typical, standard

18. resign   _____   depart, continue, desert

19. knob   _____   button, hill, dent

20. display   _____   conceal, show, relax

Name:_____ Date:_____

Antonyms: *Exercise 3*   ANTONYMS

Directions: In the following exercise choose the antonym for each of the words. Write your choice on the line.

1. innocent   _____   guilty, saintly, honest

2. plural   _____   many, often, singular

3. liquid   _____   solid, soldier, wet

4. difficult   _____   hard, simple, intense

5. die   _____   death, expire, live

6. leave   _____   depart, stay, rest

7. grumpy   _____   sad, angry, cheerful

8. surrender   _____   saved, conquer, quit

9. respect   _____   honor, contempt, rejoice

10. deny   _____   admit, defend, allow

11. work   _____   exercise, relaxation, time

12. part   _____   some, fraction, whole

13. zealous   _____   lazy, hurried, excited

14. entire   _____   all, whole, partial

15. honest   _____   true, deceitful, careful

16. fluffy   _____   stiff, plush, short

17. unify   _____   join, single, divide

18. royal   _____   noble, common, stately

19. cling   _____   grasp, abandon, silky

20. antique   _____   modern, stable, ancient

53

Name: _____ Date: _____

Antonyms: *Exercise 4* ANTONYMS

Directions: In the following exercise, choose the antonym for each of the words. Write your choice on the line.

1. right   _____   wrong, close, correct

2. yell   _____   shout, murmur, speak

3. evil   _____   lie, great, goodness

4. wisdom   _____   intelligence, folly, wise

5. worthy   _____   needy, wealthy, unworthy

6. charming   _____   repulsive, wonderful, cute

7. undivided   _____   whole, divided, complete

8. nothing   _____   something, zero, note

9. youthful   _____   happy, joyous, aged

10. confess   _____   deny, ask, tell

11. wicked   _____   evil, wise, good

12. complete   _____   finish, done, incomplete

13. sit   _____   wait, stand, save

14. round   _____   circular, oval, square

15. vocal   _____   silent, talkative, voice

16. spite   _____   meanness, truth, benevolence

17. hamper   _____   assist, prevent, store

18. virtue   _____   trip, honor, sin

19. pride   _____   vanity, humility, fear

20. escape   _____   surrender, evade, flee

Name:_____ Date:_____

Antonyms: *Exercise 5*

ANTONYMS

Directions: Write an antonym for each clue below in the crossword puzzle.

ACROSS
2. wealthy
6. joy
8. thick
11. south
12. below
14. damage
15. beautiful
16. false
18. new

DOWN
1. long
3. even
4. future
5. early
6. difficult
7. cloudy
9. peace
10. enemy
13. little
16. wide
17. best

55

Name:_____ Date:_____

Antonyms: *Exercise 6*

ANTONYMS

Directions: Write an antonym for each word. On the line below each word write a sentence using the antonym. Use a dictionary if you need help.

1. An antonym for **sharp** is _____

   _____

2. An antonym for **bumpy** is _____

   _____

3. An antonym for **forgotten** is _____

   _____

4. An antonym for **ugly** is _____

   _____

5. An antonym for **young** is _____

   _____

6. An antonym for **clean** is _____

   _____

7. An antonym for **narrow** is _____

   _____

8. An antonym for **right** is _____

   _____

9. An antonym for **sunny** is _____

   _____

10. An antonym for **simple** is _____

   _____

Name:_____ Date:_____

Antonyms: *Exercise 7*   ANTONYMS

Directions: Write an antonym for each word. On the line below each word write a sentence using the antonym. Use a dictionary if you need help.

1. An antonym for **daughter** is _____

_____

2. An antonym for **length** is _____

_____

3. An antonym for **finish** is _____

_____

4. An antonym for **lower** is _____

_____

5. An antonym for **full** is _____

_____

6. An antonym for **north** is _____

_____

7. An antonym for **silly** is _____

_____

8. An antonym for **remember** is _____

_____

9. An antonym for **find** is _____

_____

10. An antonym for **rough** is _____

_____

Name:_____ Date:_____

Antonyms: *Exercise 8*

ANTONYMS

Directions: Write an antonym for each word. On the line below each word write a sentence using the antonym. Use a dictionary if you need help.

1. An antonym for **never** is _____

_____

2. An antonym for **horrible** is _____

_____

3. An antonym for **heavy** is _____

_____

4. An antonym for **shout** is _____

_____

5. An antonym for **tidy** is _____

_____

6. An antonym for **question** is _____

_____

7. An antonym for **future** is _____

_____

8. An antonym for **buy** is _____

_____

9. An antonym for **summer** is _____

_____

10. An antonym for **wet** is _____

_____

Name:_____ Date:_____

Antonyms: *Exercise 9*

ANTONYMS

Directions: Read the following pairs of words. If they are antonyms, write yes; if they are not antonyms, write no. Use a dictionary if you need help.

1.	happy	sad	_____	19.	fact	fiction	_____
2.	punish	reward	_____	20.	ours	theirs	_____
3.	part	piece	_____	21.	dusk	dawn	_____
4.	neat	tidy	_____	22.	kind	gentle	_____
5.	clean	dirty	_____	23.	young	old	_____
6.	victory	defeat	_____	24.	fake	fraud	_____
7.	make	build	_____	25.	strike	hit	_____
8.	little	small	_____	26.	perform	act	_____
9.	common	rare	_____	27.	weak	strong	_____
10.	work	play	_____	28.	deep	shallow	_____
11.	future	past	_____	29.	wild	tame	_____
12.	school	academy	_____	30.	lose	find	_____
13.	liquid	solid	_____				
14.	narrow	wide	_____				
15.	easy	simple	_____				
16.	moist	damp	_____				
17.	part	whole	_____				
18.	east	west	_____				

Antonyms: *Exercise 10*

ANTONYMS

Name: _____ Date: _____

Directions: Read the following pairs of words. If they are antonyms, write yes; if they are not antonyms, write no. Use a dictionary if you need help.

1.	complete	finish	_____	16.	loose	tight	_____
2.	take	return	_____	17.	tow	push	_____
3.	push	pull	_____	18.	hurry	rush	_____
4.	start	begin	_____	19.	quiet	loud	_____
5.	idle	busy	_____	20.	hit	miss	_____
6.	joy	sadness	_____	21.	reply	answer	_____
7.	under	over	_____	22.	vacant	occupied	_____
8.	join	separate	_____	23.	thick	thin	_____
9.	sole	only	_____	24.	throw	pitch	_____
10.	you	me	_____	25.	bashful	bold	_____
11.	last	first	_____	26.	married	single	_____
12.	ahead	behind	_____	27.	us	them	_____
13.	inquire	ask	_____	28.	vast	huge	_____
14.	now	then	_____	29.	much	little	_____
15.	fail	succeed	_____	30.	much	some	_____

Name: _____ Date: _____

Antonyms: *Exercise 11*

ANTONYMS

Directions: Read the following pairs of words. If they are antonyms, write yes; if they are not antonyms, write no. Use a dictionary if you need help.

1. tilt   slant   _____
2. expand   contract   _____
3. end   begin   _____
4. easy   hard   _____
5. careless careful   _____
6. comical   funny   _____
7. usually   rarely   _____
8. rude   polite   _____
9. with   without   _____
10. permit   forbid   _____
11. border   edge   _____
12. desert   jungle   _____
13. here   there   _____
14. take   return   _____
15. most   least   _____

16. king   queen   _____
17. alike   same   _____
18. dishonest honest   _____
19. easy   simple   _____
20. cool   warm   _____
21. command order   _____
22. scream   whisper   _____
23. choose   select   _____
24. outer   inner   _____
25. chase   pursue   _____
26. swift   slow   _____
27. gain   loss   _____
28. empty   full   _____
29. break   shatter   _____
30. sour   tart   _____

61

Name: _____ Date: _____

Antonyms: *Exercise 12*

ANTONYMS

Directions: Read each of the following sentences. Choose the correct antonym for the underlined word from the word bank and write it on the line. Use a dictionary if you need help.

solid	even	nervous	rare	seek
raw	defeat	guilty	single	peace
below	fake	queen	there	noisy

1. Before a test I am not <u>calm</u>; I am _____.

2. There are very few people who want <u>war</u>; most people want _____.

3. Some days we work the <u>odd</u> problems in math and some days the _____.

4. The jury had to decide if the person on trial was <u>innocent</u> or _____.

5. Matt's books were left <u>here</u> and his jacket was left _____.

6. Most pennies are <u>common</u>, but an 1877 Indian head penny is very _____.

7. In England there is a <u>king</u> or a _____.

8. Laura's brother is <u>married</u>, but she is _____.

9. Sarah has <u>real</u> leather shoes, but a _____ fur jacket.

10. In the library they want you to be <u>quiet</u>. They will tell you if you are too _____.

11. In bunk beds, do you like to sleep <u>above</u> or _____?

12. I prefer my meat <u>cooked</u>, but my dog prefers hers _____.

13. Our team had a <u>victory</u> in the first two games, but a _____ in the last one.

14. Water goes into the freezer a <u>liquid</u> and comes out a _____.

15. The kids in the neighborhood play <u>hide</u> and _____.

Name: _____ Date: _____

Antonyms: *Exercise 13*

ANTONYMS

Directions: Read each of the following sentences. Choose the correct antonym for the under-lined word from the word bank and write it on the line. Use a dictionary if you need help.

go	interesting	forget	lend	tight
those	polite	give	cold	answer
present	listen	slow	invisible	defend

1. Are you going to buy <u>these</u> shoes or _____?

2. I never <u>borrow</u> money, but I always _____ it.

3. Hal would like to <u>remain</u> at ball practice, but he has to _____ home.

4. I like my soup <u>hot</u> and my lemonade _____.

5. John was gone from class, so he was marked <u>absent</u>; everyone else was _____.

6. Mom will <u>tell</u> me things to do, but I don't always _____.

7. Susie is a <u>fast</u> runner, but a _____ swimmer.

8. If aliens did <u>attack</u>, how would we _____ our world?

9. Do you <u>remember</u> the dates on the history test? I sometimes _____ them.

10. Boy, Caroline was really <u>rude</u>. I thought she was more _____ than that.

11. Rusty's collar can't be too <u>loose</u> or too _____.

12. Mrs. Evans said to <u>take</u> the notes home and _____ them to your parents.

13. In the game of Jeopardy you have to know the <u>question</u> rather than the _____.

14. Some television shows are really <u>boring</u> and others are very _____.

15. I know I am always <u>visible</u>, but some days it would be fun to be _____.

Antonyms: *Exercise 14*

ANTONYMS

Directions: Read each of the following sentences. Choose the correct antonym for the underlined word from the word bank and write it on the line. Use a dictionary if you need help.

straight	sad	sunny	heavy	sharp
open	right	dangerous	dirty	thin
quiet	sour	serious	East	careful

1. I am not <u>happy</u> today; I feel _____.

2. We are not vacationing in the <u>West</u>; we will be in the _____.

3. I do not write with my <u>left</u> hand; I write with my _____ hand.

4. Bill's sister is not <u>foolish</u>; she is _____.

5. Laura's dad is not <u>fat</u>; he is _____.

6. Be careful. The knife is not <u>dull</u>; it is _____.

7. Ben, don't be <u>clumsy</u> carrying the glass; please be _____.

8. That pot doesn't look <u>clean</u>; it looks _____.

9. I heard it won't be <u>cloudy</u> tomorrow; it will be _____.

10. Wow, that candy isn't <u>sweet</u>; it is _____.

11. Mrs. Brown told our class not to be <u>noisy</u>; we are to be _____.

12. Playing with fireworks isn't <u>safe</u>; it is _____.

13. Those bags of sand aren't <u>light</u>; they are _____.

14. After braces my teeth aren't <u>crooked</u>; they are _____.

15. Keep the back door <u>closed</u>; don't leave it _____.

Antonyms: *Exercise 15*

ANTONYMS

Directions: Choose a word from the word bank and write the correct antonym for the word in parentheses in the blank. Use a dictionary if you need help.

thickest	valuable	younger	lost	sunny
wild	strongest	cruel	raw	tell
interesting	repaired	queen	most	building

1. My sister _____ (found) her charm bracelet.

2. Our class is going to see the _____ (tame) animals in the zoo.

3. I think it is _____ (kind) to make fun of other students.

4. The construction company is _____ (destroying) a new office building.

5. Sam has the _____ (least) brothers and sisters in our class.

6. Carri was crowned _____ (king) of the parade.

7. The weather forecaster promised that it would be _____ (cloudy) tomorrow.

8. Michael has a _____ (older) sister.

9. The recipe for cookies calls for two _____ (cooked) eggs.

10. Have you ever _____ (damaged) a zipper before?

11. Jeffrey won the _____ (weakest) boy contest.

12. That diamond necklace looks _____ (worthless) to me.

13. Could you _____ (listen) those people to be quiet?

14. The movie we saw last week was really _____ (boring).

15. Give Dad the _____ (thinnest) piece of cake.

Name: _____ Date: _____

Antonyms: *Exercise 16* ANTONYMS

Directions: Choose a word from the word bank and write the correct antonym for the word in parentheses in the blank. Use a dictionary if you need help.

wrong	joy	brave	many	South
inner	raise	rarely	succeed	dawn
work	like	future	under	shallow

1. The knight was very _____ (timid) when he faced the dragon.

2. Pat hoped to _____ (fail) in the swimming meet.

3. Elizabeth felt great _____ (sorrow) when she saw the "A" on her test.

4. Dad and Mom have to go to _____ (play) every day.

5. On Twin Day at school we all try to dress _____ (different) a friend.

6. You need to _____ (lower) your hand to ask a question in class.

7. Do you think outer space will be our home in the _____ (past)?

8. When you first learn to swim, it is a good idea to stay in the _____ (deep) water.

9. Submarines travel _____ (above) the surface of the water.

10. Steven marked seven math problems _____ (right) on my paper.

11. We like to float down the river on an _____ (outer) tube.

12. Tom _____ (usually) brings his lunch to school.

13. Our science class met at _____ (dusk) to watch the sunrise.

14. The coach had _____ (few) people try out for the team.

15. Carl just got back from a trip to the _____ (North).

66

Name: _____ Date: _____

Antonyms: *Exercise 17*

ANTONYMS

Directions: Choose a word from the word bank and write the correct antonym for the word in parentheses in the blank. Use a dictionary if you need help.

added	**mother**	**specific**	**poor**	**beginning**
knowledge	**discard**	**some**	**noon**	**thankful**
sharp	**country**	**accepted**	**clean**	**morning**

1. At Thanksgiving we collect food for the _____ (rich).

2. The kittens all ran to the _____ (father) cat.

3. I always like to start a book at the _____ (end).

4. My mother said I had to _____ (keep) all the junk on my floor.

5. Tim _____ (refused) the invitation to go to the baseball game with his neighbor.

6. Isn't it nice to sleep on nice _____ (dirty) sheets and pillowcases?

7. My uncle is a farmer in the _____ (city).

8. Amanda was so _____ (ungrateful) when she got the lead in the play.

9. We needed more chairs when we _____ (subtracted) two people to our lunch table.

10. Mrs. Klimstra wanted _____ (vague) answers for the history questions.

11. I hate to get up to go to school in the _____ (night).

12. Be careful in archery; the arrows have _____ (blunt) tips.

13. Dad wants us to save _____ (none) of the apple pie for him.

14. Mrs. Meyer told us _____ (ignorance) will take us far in life.

15. We get to eat lunch at _____ (midnight).

Name:_____ Date:_____

Antonyms: *Exercise 18*

ANTONYMS

Directions: Write an antonym for each clue below in the crossword puzzle.

	ACROSS		DOWN
5.	scream	1.	never
7.	hot	2.	tender
8.	dirty	3.	vacant
11.	expensive	4.	white
12.	father	6.	usually
14.	victory	9.	deny
16.	nervous	10.	discard
17.	city	13.	learn
18.	wealthy	15.	fact

Name: _____ Date: _____

Antonyms: *Exercise 19*   ANTONYMS

Directions: In the blank following the sentence, write an antonym for the underlined word. Use a dictionary if you need help.

1. My piece of meat was very <u>tough</u>. _____

2. I don't think we will ever get this math project <u>started</u>. _____

3. Is your sister <u>married</u>? _____

4. Would you loop that <u>under</u> the other piece of yarn for me? _____

5. Whenever we get in the car, the gas tank seems to be <u>full</u>. _____

6. Michelle said she would meet us <u>there</u>. _____

7. This new gum is really <u>sweet</u>. _____

8. Who is the <u>king</u> of England right now? _____

9. Gayle always has such a <u>sullen</u> look on her face. _____

10. Dad has starch put in his shirts because they are <u>stiff</u>. _____

11. Chris wants you to <u>leave</u>. _____

12. Bill looks so <u>calm</u> standing on the stage. _____

13. This had to be the <u>best</u> day of my life. _____

14. I think I will wear the <u>fancy</u> sweater to school today. _____

15. Look at that <u>tiny</u> bug crawling across the sidewalk. _____

Name: _____ Date: _____

Antonyms: *Exercise 20*

ANTONYMS

Directions: In the blank following the sentence, write an antonym for the underlined word. Use a dictionary if you need help.

1. The new bleacher seats felt very <u>rough</u> when I sat on them. _____

2. Stephanie wants to borrow <u>those</u> shoes. _____

3. I think this chair is <u>vacant</u>. _____

4. Are you going to be <u>idle</u> on Saturday afternoon? _____

5. Because of my last name, I am always seated in the <u>last</u> seat in the room. _____

6. How many of the tennis games did you <u>lose</u>? _____

7. Mrs. White has always wanted to take a trip to the <u>desert</u>. _____

8. Abracadabra, the rabbit <u>appeared</u>. _____

9. Are there many <u>tame</u> animals in the zoo? _____

10. If you don't behave in the classroom, you have to <u>sit</u> in the hall. _____

11. Are we supposed to do the <u>even</u> problems in math? _____

12. If we <u>divide</u> the number by six, I think we will get the correct answer. _____

13. Allison picked <u>light</u> purple for the flag. _____

14. Do you think this coin is very <u>common</u>? _____

15. That warrior looks very <u>fearful</u>. _____

Name: _____ Date: _____

Antonyms: *Exercise 21*

ANTONYMS

Directions: Write an antonym for each clue below in the crossword puzzle.

	ACROSS		DOWN
5.	some	1.	mine
7.	achieve	2.	dry
9.	huge	3.	desert
10.	all	4.	multiply
11.	round	6.	accept
12.	sharp	8.	add
13.	dusk	10.	something
14.	sound	11.	married
15.	specific	16.	swift
16.	stop		
17.	ignorance		

Name: _____ Date: _____

Antonyms: *Exercise 22*

ANTONYMS

Directions: In each of the following sentences, choose the letter of the antonym of the under-lined word and write the letter on the blank. Use a dictionary if necessary.

_____ 1. The lion in the story was very <u>timid</u>.

(a) shy   (b) courageous   (c) careful

_____ 2. You shouldn't be <u>wasteful</u> when you share your candy.

(a) stingy   (b) wishful   (c) messy

_____ 3. The hurricane in the Gulf of Mexico was a <u>gentle</u> storm.

(a) kind   (b) huge   (c) violent

_____ 4. The <u>clear</u> glass bottle once held medicine used during Colonial times.

(a) opaque   (b) brown   (c) clean

_____ 5. John is very <u>vain</u> about his acting accomplishments.

(a) happy   (b) excited   (c) modest

_____ 6. The ambulance paramedics <u>leisurely</u> worked at the car accident.

(a) urgently   (b) carefully   (c) slowly

_____ 7. The kings of England would come back to their castles and boast of their <u>defeats</u>.

(a) destinies   (b) triumphs   (c) failures

_____ 8. Laura <u>carelessly</u> put all the books on the shelf.

(a) cautiously   (b) meticulously   (c) quickly

_____ 9. The politician on television was talking about a <u>conservative</u> plan to save animals.

(a) liberal   (b) complex   (c) likeable

_____ 10. Brian <u>collected</u> the feed in the yak's pen.

(a) planted   (b) scattered   (c) watered

Name:_____ Date:_____

Antonyms: *Exercise 23*

ANTONYMS

Directions: In each of the following sentences, choose the letter of the antonym of the under-lined word and write the letter on the blank. Use a dictionary if necessary.

_____ 1. The photographer asked the children to <u>grimace</u> for the camera.

  (a) smile   (b) frown   (c) scowl

_____ 2. It was a <u>normal</u> day when the clown walked into our classroom.

  (a) regular   (b) strange   (c) sunny

_____ 3. For some parts in a play you have to <u>disrobe</u> in character.

  (a) act   (b) sing   (c) dress

_____ 4. Chris and Matt <u>angrily</u> carried the boxes of supplies for Mrs. Weed.

  (a) happily   (b) sullenly   (c) quickly

_____ 5. Those two girls were very <u>friendly</u> when we first met them.

  (a) closely   (b) aloof   (c) kind

_____ 6. Hank sat <u>cheerfully</u> outside the principal's office.

  (a) laughingly   (b) suddenly   (c) sullenly

_____ 7. Mrs. Evans said we had to settle this argument <u>combatively</u>.

  (a) peacefully   (b) badly   (c) soon

_____ 8. My grandma is always telling me to wear <u>foolish</u> shoes.

  (a) new   (b) white   (c) sensible

_____ 9. Our school spirit committee said we were not to <u>cheer</u> at basketball games.

  (a) boo   (b) listen   (c) play

_____ 10. Ruth <u>casually</u> picked out what she would wear to the awards ceremony.

  (a) quickly   (b) carefully   (c) yesterday

Name: _____ Date: _____

Antonyms: *Exercise 24*

ANTONYMS

Directions: In each of the following sentences, choose the letter of the antonym of the underlined word and write the letter on the blank. Use a dictionary if necessary.

_____ 1. We need to <u>decrease</u> the number of members in our club if we want to continue meeting.

     (a) decline   (b) increase   (c) lose

_____ 2. Heather was very <u>clumsy</u> when she did her gymnastics routine.

     (a) agile   (b) awkward   (c) happy

_____ 3. Kansas is known for its <u>undulating</u> highways.

     (a) rolling   (b) flat   (c) wide

_____ 4. My savings account seems to be <u>increasing</u> every time I go to the bank.

     (a) growing   (b) empty   (c) dwindling

_____ 5. Mr. Meyer <u>reproachfully</u> listened to our debate on school uniforms.

     (a) approvingly   (b) angrily   (c) carefully

_____ 6. In our town, the roads <u>improve</u> after a winter of freeze and thaw, freeze and thaw.

     (a) clean   (b) deteriorate   (c) defend

_____ 7. The mother rabbit became very <u>calm</u> when she saw the cat going toward the bunny.

     (a) quiet   (b) happy   (c) agitated

_____ 8. The model had an <u>ordinary</u> appearance.

     (a) striking   (b) plain   (c) careful

_____ 9. My mom gave me a really <u>lenient</u> curfew for school nights.

     (a) level   (b) easy   (c) strict

_____ 10. The team looked <u>dismal</u> as it waited for the results of the replay.

     (a) sad   (b) hopeful   (c) angry

Name: _____ Date: _____

Antonyms: *Exercise 25*

ANTONYMS

Directions: Use each of the following fragments in a complete sentence. Then write the sentence again using the antonym of the underlined word. Make sure that your sentence will make sense. Use a dictionary if necessary.

1. most <u>exciting</u>

    _____

    _____

2. the <u>exciting</u> play

    _____

    _____

3. <u>stay</u>, please

    _____

    _____

4. in this time of <u>peace</u>

    _____

    _____

5. <u>above</u> the tall green grass

    _____

    _____

6. <u>nervous</u> at first

    _____

    _____

7. the <u>old</u> chair

    _____

    _____

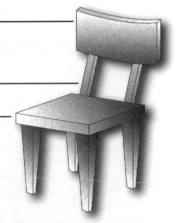

Name: _____ Date: _____

Antonyms: *Exercise 26*

ANTONYMS

Directions: Use each of the following fragments in a complete sentence. Then write the sentence again using the antonym of the underlined word. Make sure that your sentence will make sense. Use a dictionary if necessary.

1. the <u>young</u> woman

   _____

   _____

2. the <u>morning</u> of our trip

   _____

   _____

3. look <u>up</u>

   _____

   _____

4. the <u>honest</u> crook

   _____

   _____

5. the team's <u>victories</u>

   _____

   _____

6. the <u>loose</u> necktie

   _____

   _____

7. on my <u>sister's</u> birthday

   _____

   _____

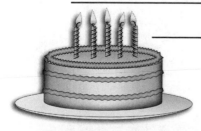

Antonyms: *Exercise 27*

ANTONYMS

Directions: Use each of the following fragments in a complete sentence. Then write the sentence again using the antonym of the underlined word. Make sure that your sentence will make sense. Use a dictionary if necessary.

1. the <u>sadness</u> in their eyes

   _____

   _____

2. the <u>wide</u> box

   _____

   _____

3. on a <u>cloudy</u> day

   _____

   _____

4. if you <u>deny</u>

   _____

   _____

5. will <u>thaw</u>

   _____

   _____

6. in the <u>future</u>

   _____

   _____

7. the <u>friendly</u> dog

   _____

   _____

Name: _____ Date: _____

Antonyms: *Exercise 28*

ANTONYMS

Directions: Some words have more than one antonym. Choose from the word bank the antonyms for the words below. Write the antonyms on the lines below the word.

sloppy	above	arrive	occupied	help	flat
true	faithful	aid	light	rough	remain
handicap	answer	few	poorly	discard	messy
abandon	buoyant	smooth	meager	disadvantage	courage
bravery	full	badly	respond	over	hard

advantage

_____

_____

under

_____

_____

soft

_____

_____

bumpy

_____

false

_____

empty

_____

_____

perfectly

_____

_____

leave

_____

_____

heavy

_____

receive

_____

neat

_____

_____

ask

_____

_____

fear

_____

_____

prevent

_____

many

_____

Antonyms: *Exercise 29*

ANTONYMS

Directions: Some words have more than one antonym. Choose from the word bank the antonyms for the words below. Write the antonyms on the lines below the word.

mannerly	straight	pale	short	aware	certain
uneven	dirty	beneath	forget	polite	irregular
cruel	intelligent	specific	loss	soiled	war
colorless	square	stubby	rough	defeat	answer
conflict	light	ignore	bright	reply	under

victory

_____

_____

over

_____

_____

vague

_____

_____

ignorant

_____

_____

question

_____

_____

tall

_____

_____

rude

_____

_____

clean

_____

_____

kind

_____

_____

peace

_____

_____

colorful

_____

_____

round

_____

_____

equal

_____

_____

remember

_____

_____

dark

_____

_____

Name:_____ Date:_____

Antonyms: *Exercise 30*

ANTONYMS

Directions: Some words have more than one antonym. Choose from the word bank the antonyms for the words below. Write the antonyms on the lines below the word.

easy	weighty	large	repair	destroy
hard	kind	play	friend	seldom
deep	simple	late	bottomless	heavy
tough	fix	rarely	tardy	ruin
ally	leisure	loud	expensive	big
retain	gentle	keep	costly	noisy

discard

_____

_____

work

_____

_____

stern

_____

_____

shallow

_____

_____

quiet

_____

_____

little

_____

_____

create

_____

_____

damage

_____

_____

early

_____

_____

enemy

_____

_____

light

_____

_____

often

_____

_____

difficult

_____

_____

tender

_____

_____

cheap

_____

_____

Name: _____   Date: _____

Antonyms: *Exercise 31*   ANTONYMS

Directions: Rewrite the following paragraph, changing each underlined word to its antonym.

Mrs. <u>White's</u> class looked <u>happy</u>. They had just heard Mrs. <u>White</u> <u>yell</u> that there would be a <u>short</u> test tomorrow. Sarah was especially <u>happy</u> because she never had <u>failed</u> a test before. <u>None</u> of her <u>foes</u> decided that they would study for the test. They <u>told</u> Sarah to come too. Hopefully this time when Sarah took the test things would be the <u>same</u>.

<u>Yesterday</u> arrived and Sarah was <u>calm</u>. She <u>wrote</u> the directions at the <u>bottom</u> of the page and <u>ended</u> the test. She hoped she had done <u>poorly.</u>

When the grades came, Sarah was <u>unhappy</u>. She had finally <u>failed</u> one of Mrs. <u>White's</u> tests!

Name: _____ Date: _____

Antonyms: *Exercise 32*

ANTONYMS

Directions: For each sentence below, decide if it has two synonyms or antonyms. Underline the synonyms or antonyms. Write **S** on the blank space for synonym or **A** for antonym.

_____ 1. The bus schedule told of the arrival and departure times of the buses.

_____ 2. My younger brother can annoy and irritate me.

_____ 3. You need to look at the science experiment and observe the molecules.

_____ 4. I dropped a glass on the floor; it broke and shattered into a million pieces.

_____ 5. I don't want a piece of cake that is too big or too little.

_____ 6. I'd like to think this baseball card is genuine, but I think it's fake.

_____ 7. I think my sister is pretty, but her boyfriend tells her she's beautiful.

_____ 8. Bill tried to be careful with the paint; I knew he would be cautious.

_____ 9. Put the plants on the edge of the garden; I want it to be a border.

_____ 10. When my dad fishes, he catches the fish and then releases them.

_____ 11. You are a great friend; you have stayed through thick and thin.

_____ 12. I wish you wouldn't yell or shout to your friends.

_____ 13. To knit, you put the yarn under and over the needle.

_____ 14. I think some of those flowers look like these flowers.

_____ 15. Laura, is that sweater yours or mine?

_____ 16. Leave your book here and retrieve it later.

_____ 17. Close the window and open the door.

_____ 18. I will call the school and phone your parents.

_____ 19. Don't forget your lunch; remember it is in the refrigerator.

_____ 20. If you don't hurry, we will have to rush to get there on time.

Name: _____ Date: _____

Antonyms: *Exercise 33*

ANTONYMS

Directions: For each sentence below, decide if it has two synonyms or antonyms. Underline the synonyms or antonyms. Write **S** on the blank space for synonym or **A** for antonym.

_____ 1. The sick woman was tired and weary.

_____ 2. Do you have enough money to buy anything? What will you purchase?

_____ 3. I can't tell if the pudding is a solid or a liquid.

_____ 4. Wow, you look calm. I am so nervous.

_____ 5. Jack was fearless when that dog growled; he is so brave.

_____ 6. Barb is studying abroad. I'd like to go overseas sometime.

_____ 7. Where is the entry to the school? I need to find the door.

_____ 8. That was so easy. I didn't think it would be so simple.

_____ 9. The dog ate the cooked and the raw hamburgers.

_____ 10. Does England have a king or a queen now?

_____ 11. Did you play hide and seek when you were outside?

_____ 12. When will this play finish? It should have come to the end by now.

_____ 13. Just rake the leaves in a pile; put them in one big heap in the backyard.

_____ 14. The lemonade looks cool and frosty.

_____ 15. Did you scream or shriek on the roller coaster?

_____ 16. We will stop at the store and then go home.

_____ 17. Can you see any smoke or hear the alarm?

_____ 18. The friendly puppy nuzzled the grumpy lady.

_____ 19. After finding the squirrel in the trap, we put it in a cage.

_____ 20. Who left the window open and the door unlocked?

Antonyms: *Antonym List*   ANTONYMS

above - below

above - under

absent - present

accept - refuse

achieve - fail

acute - obtuse

add - subtract

advantage - disadvantage

advantage - handicap

adverse - favorable

ahead - behind

aid - prevent

all - none

ally - enemy

angrily - happily

antique - modern

apart - together

argue - agree

ask - answer

ask - respond

assent - dissent

assert - deny

attack - defend

aware - ignorant

back - front

bashful - bold

beautiful - ugly

begin - end

beneath - over

best - worst

big - little

blunt - sharp

boring - exciting

boring - interesting

borrow - lend

brave - fearful

bright - dark

bumpy - flat

bumpy - smooth

buy - sell

cage - release

calm - agitated

calm - nervous

careless - careful

carelessly - meticulously

casually - carefully

cause - effect

charming - repulsive

cheap - costly

cheap - expensive

cheer - boo

cheerfully - sullenly

city - country

clean - dirty

clean - soiled

clear - opaque

cling - abandon

closed - open

cloudy - sunny

clumsy - agile

clumsy - careful

collected - scattered

colorful - colorless

colorful - pale

colossal - tiny

combatively - peacefully

common - rare

complete - incomplete

confess - ask

confess - deny

conservative - liberal

cooked - raw

cool - warm

corny - cool

costly - cheap

courage - fear

create - destroy

create - ruin

crooked - straight

damage - fix

damage - repair

dark - bright

dark - light

decrease - increase

deep - shallow

defeat - triumph

deny - admit

desert - jungle

destroy - create

destroying - building

die - live

different - like

difficult - easy

difficult - simple

dirty - clean

discard - keep

discard - retain

dishonest - honest

dismal - hopeful

Antonyms: *Antonym List*

ANTONYMS

display - conceal
disrobe - dress
dry - wet
dull - sharp
dull - shiny
dusk - dawn
early - late
east - west
easy - hard
empty - full
empty - occupied
end - begin
end - beginning
enemy - ally
enemy - friend
entire - partial
equal - uneven
equal - irregular
escape - surrender
even - odd
evil - goodness
expand - contract
expensive - cheap
fact - fiction
fail - succeed
fake - fraud
false - faithful
false - true
fast - slow
fat - thin
father - mother
fear - bravery
fear - courage

feeble - strong
few - many
fierce - gentle
first - last
fluffy - stiff
foolish - sensible
foolish - serious
forget - remember
found - lost
friendly - aloof
future - past
gain - loss
gather - scatter
gentle - violent
graceful - clumsy
grimace - smile
grumpy - cheerful
hamper - assist
handicap - advantage
happy - sad
happy - unhappy
hard - soft
hard - tender
harsh - mild
heavy - buoyant
heavy - light
help - prevent
here - there
hide - seek
hit - miss
honest - deceitful
honest - dishonest
hot - cold

huge - tiny
idle - busy
ignorance - knowledge
ignorant - aware
ignorant - intelligent
improve - deteriorate
increasing - decreasing
increasing - dwindling
inhale - exhale
innocent - guilty
join - separate
joy - sadness
keep - discard
kind - cruel
king - queen
knob - dent
large - little
large - small
last - first
late - early
lead - follow
learn - teach
least - most
leave - arrive
leave - remain
leave - stay
left - right
length - width
lenient - strict
leisurely - urgently
life - death
light - dark
light - heavy

Antonyms: *Antonym List*

ANTONYMS

limp - stiff	odd - even	quiet - noisy
liquid - solid	often - rarely	raise - lower
listen - tell	often - seldom	rarely - often
little - big	old - new	raw - cooked
little - large	older - younger	real - fake
long - short	ordinary - striking	receive - abandon
loose - tight	ours - theirs	receive - discard
lose - find	outer - inner	refused - accepted
lower - raise	over - beneath	remain - go
lower - upper	over - under	remember - forget
mannerly - rude	part - whole	reply - question
many - few	past - future	reproachfully - approvingly
married - single	peace - conflict	resign - continue
midnight - noon	peace - war	respect - contempt
mine - yours	perfectly - badly	respond - ask
most - least	perfectly - poorly	respond - question
much - little	permit - forbid	retain - discard
much - some	plain - fancy	rich - poor
multiply - divide	play - work	right - left
narrow - wide	plural - singular	right - wrong
neat - messy	polite - rude	rough - smooth
neat - sloppy	poorly - well	round - square
nervous - calm	prevent - aid	round - thin
never - always	prevent - help	royal - common
new - old	pride - humility	rude - mannerly
night - morning	punish - reward	rude - polite
noisy - quiet	pupil - teacher	safe - dangerous
none - some	push - pull	scream - whisper
normal - strange	question - answer	seldom - often
normal - unusual	question - reply	shallow - deep
north - south	question - response	shallow - bottomless
nothing - something	quick - slow	short - tall
now - then	quiet - loud	sick - well

Antonyms: *Antonym List*

ANTONYMS

sit - stand
smooth - rough
soft - hard
soft - rough
some - none
something - nothing
sorrow - joy
sound - silence
south - north
specific - vague
spite - benevolence
square - round
start - stop
stay - go
stern - kind
stern - gentle
stop - start
straight - round
stubby - tall
subtracted - added
sullen - cheerful
surrender - conquer
sweet - sour
swift - slow
take - give
take - return
tall - short
tall - stubby
tame - wild
tardy - early
tear - mend
tell - ask
tell - listen

tender - tough
thankful - ungrateful
thaw - freeze
these - those
thick - thin
tidy - messy
thinnest - thickest
timid - bold
timid - brave
timid - courageous
tired - rested
tow - push
triumph - defeat
ugly - pretty
under - above
under - over
undivided - divided
undulating - flat
ungrateful - thankful
unify - divide
urgent - leisurely
us - them
useless - useful
usually - rarely
vacant - occupied
vague - certain
vague - specific
vain - modest
vanish - appear
victory - defeat
victory - loss
violent - gentle
virtue - sin

visible - invisible
vocal - silent
vulgar - refined
wait - act
wander - stay
war - peace
wary - careless
wasteful - stingy
weak - strong
weakest - strongest
wealth - poverty
wealthy - poor
west - east
white - black
whole - part
wicked - good
wide - narrow
wild - tame
wisdom - folly
with - without
work - leisure
work - play
work - relaxation
worthless - valuable
worthy - unworthy
yell - murmur
yell - whisper
you - me
young - old
youthful - aged
zealous - lazy

Answer Keys

Synonyms: Exercise 1
(p. 2)

1. damp	11. neat
2. hat	12. happy
3. home	13. assist
4. bright	14. talk
5. jump	15. gazed
6. little	16. path
7. yell	17. shore
8. throw	18. spin
9. enemy	19. cry
10. stop	20. quiet

Synonyms: Exercise 2
(p. 3)

1. glad	11. litter
2. visitor	12. absent
3. finish	13. give
4. easy	14. mistake
5. spin	15. cried
6. quick	16. silly
7. stroll	17. toppled
8. funny	18. close
9. loud	19. rich
10. pull	20. repair

Synonyms: Exercise 3
(p. 4)

1. burn	11. receive
2. bold	12. awkward
3. perform	13. edge
4. ask	14. refuse
5. cut	15. select
6. break	16. risky
7. find	17. cheap
8. avoid	18. polite
9. same	19. chase
10. only	20. order

Synonyms: Exercise 4
(p. 5)

1. defeat
2. perhaps
3. rough
4. ordinary
5. dawdle
6. enthusiastic
7. illness
8. amaze
9. occur
10. door
11. thick
12. result
13. seize
14. weary
15. vacant
16. discharge
17. buy
18. residence
19. inquire
20. normal

Synonyms: Exercise 5
(p. 6)

1. fib
2. trip
3. timid
4. leave
5. purchase
6. pick
7. absent
8. carve
9. awards
10. vacant
11. ache
12. gentle
13. flavor
14. laughed
15. ill

Synonyms: Exercise 6
(p. 7)

1. scampered
2. shattered
3. shoved
4. beach
5. guests
6. rush
7. pause
8. hopped
9. street
10. friends
11. annoy
12. raise
13. quit
14. cooperate
15. gather

Synonyms: Exercise 7
(p. 8)

1. health
2. frown
3. serious
4. fellow
5. joyful
6. excited
7. race
8. type
9. starve
10. excited
11. sad
12. inform
13. inspect
14. idle
15. start
16. tardy
17. major
18. talk
19. stern
20. pitch

Synonyms: Exercise 8
(p. 9)

1. under
2. friend
3. mural
4. quickly
5. wilted
6. shining
7. rushing
8. fearful
9. sled
10. much
11. mountain
12. shop
13. curious
14. visor
15. ripe
16. tip
17. tough
18. clearly
19. spell
20. chicken

Synonyms: Exercise 9
(p. 10)

Synonyms: Exercise 12
(p. 13)

1. no	16. yes
2. yes	17. no
3. yes	18. yes
4. yes	19. yes
5. no	20. no
6. yes	21. yes
7. no	22. yes
8. yes	23. yes
9. no	24. yes
10. yes	25. yes
11. yes	26. no
12. no	27. yes
13. yes	28. yes
14. no	29. no
15. yes	30. no

Synonyms: Exercise 13
(p. 14)

1. no	16. yes
2. yes	17. yes
3. no	18. yes
4. yes	19. no
5. yes	20. yes
6. yes	21. no
7. no	22. yes
8. yes	23. no
9. yes	24. yes
10. yes	25. no
11. yes	26. yes
12. yes	27. no
13. no	28. yes
14. yes	29. no
15. yes	30. no

Synonyms: Exercise 14
(p. 15)

1. no	16. yes
2. yes	17. yes
3. yes	18. yes
4. no	19. yes
5. yes	20. no
6. yes	21. yes
7. yes	22. no
8. no	23. yes
9. yes	24. yes
10. no	25. no
11. yes	26. yes
12. yes	27. no
13. yes	28. yes
14. yes	29. no
15. yes	30. yes

Answer Keys

Synonyms: Exercise 15 (p. 16)
1. rage
2. ache
3. idle
4. ill
5. remain
6. mistake
7. perhaps
8. stroll
9. below
10. connect
11. brook
12. swift
13. wealthy
14. comical
15. unhappy

Synonyms: Exercise 16 (p. 17)
1. sly
2. vanished
3. admit
4. pull
5. flavor
6. complete
7. vow
8. repair
9. cut
10. finished
11. hare
12. just
13. entry
14. same
15. piece

Synonyms: Exercise 17 (p. 18)
1. brag
2. start
3. huge
4. smell
5. interior
6. collect
7. build
8. purchase
9. increase
10. grin
11. award
12. perform
13. odd
14. awkward
15. tired

Synonyms: Exercise 18 (p. 19)
1. equal
2. tasks
3. odor
4. wound
5. explosion
6. vacant
7. decline
8. litter
9. tart
10. assist
11. noisy
12. error
13. consent
14. vanished
15. tidy

Synonyms: Exercise 19 (p. 20)
1. parfait
2. chat
3. stolen
4. synthetic
5. affectionate
6. fiesta
7. substitute
8. trustworthy
9. dampen
10. ethical
11. succeeded
12. desired
13. zero
14. mysterious
15. forever

Synonyms: Exercise 20 (p. 21)

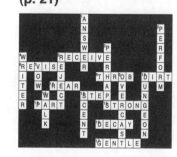

Synonyms: Exercise 23 (p. 24)

Synonyms: Exercise 24 (p. 25)
1. a   8. c
2. c   9. a
3. a   10. b
4. b   11. a
5. c   12. b
6. a   13. a
7. b

Synonyms: Exercise 25 (p. 26)
1. a   8. b
2. b   9. b
3. c   10. c
4. c   11. a
5. a   12. c
6. b   13. a
7. a

Synonyms: Exercise 26 (p. 27)
1. a   8. c
2. b   9. a
3. a   10. b
4. b   11. a
5. c   12. b
6. a   13. b
7. b

Synonyms: Exercise 29 (p. 31)
1. stalking
2. floating
3. excited
4. piece
5. plain
6. labor
7. carve
8. journey

9. mysterious
10. collects
11. repair
12. tardy
13. frowned
14. fell
15. inflate

Synonyms: Exercise 34 (p. 38)
1. young
2. forgetful
3. enemy
4. happy
5. laugh
6. moan
7. perhaps
8. simplify
9. thrive
10. dubious
11. open
12. view
13. brutal
14. continuing
15. rip

Synonyms: Exercise 35 (p. 39)
1. appease
2. robust
3. honest
4. shapeless
5. logical
6. stop
7. expand
8. imprudent
9. yank
10. dirty
11. lose
12. deflate
13. play
14. calm
15. truant

Synonyms: Exercise 36 (p. 40)
1. vapor
2. destroy
3. remain
4. continue
5. evil
6. crowd

2. failure
3. occupied
9. uneven
10. release
11. wait
12. advanced
13. active
14. deprive
15. entire

Synonyms: Exercise 37 (p. 41)

discuss:	debate
	dispute
	argue
	explain
afraid:	nervous
	anxious
	frightened
	fearful
brave:	daring
	fearless
	heroic
	valiant
yell:	bellow
	cry
	shriek
	shout
bend:	twist
	deform
	round
	buckle
friend:	pal
	chum
	comrade
	playmate
soft:	smooth
	downy
	silky
	delicate
meet:	convene
	assemble
	associate
	unite
fear:	terror
	fright
	anxiety
	dread

Synonyms: Exercise 38 (p. 42)

loud:	booming
	noise
	resonant
	deafening
connect:	join
	combine
	unite
	attach
wet:	moist
	sodden
	damp
	soaked
trash:	litter
	garbage
	refuse
	waste
only:	single
	wholly
	totally
	unique
buy:	purchase
	acquire
	redeem
	procure
sick:	ill
	diseased
	infirm
	invalid
boast:	brag
	flaunt
	gloat
	bluster
catch:	snatch
	grab
	seize
	capture

Synonyms: Exercise 39 (p. 43)

celebration:	festival
	holiday
	jubilee
	anniversary
sell:	market
	vend
	auction
	exchange

important:	principal
	essential
	significant
	great
pretty:	cute
	attractive
	lovely
	beautiful
occasionally:	
	infrequently
	hardly
	seldom
	irregularly
strict:	stringent
	austere
	stern
	severe
happily:	merrily
	gladly
	joyfully
	laughingly
flat:	level
	horizontal
	smooth
	even
cool:	frigid
	nippy
	chill
	frosty

Antonyms: Exercise 1 (p. 51)

1.	rough	11.	front
2.	messy	12.	rested
3.	ask	13.	sell
4.	last	14.	sad
5.	over	15.	shiny
6.	well	16.	early
7.	fiction	17.	short
8.	narrow	18.	full
9.	cruel	19.	quiet
10.	end	20.	go

Antonyms: Exercise 2 (p. 52)

1. none
2. tough
3. keep
4. invisible
5. whisper
6. yours

7. seek
8. defend
9. late
10. shallow
11. seldom
12. stiff
13. fail
14. first
15. vague
16. release
17. unusual
18. continue
19. dent
20. conceal

Antonyms: Exercise 3 (p. 53)

1. guilty
2. singular
3. solid
4. simple
5. live
6. stay
7. cheerful
8. conquer
9. contempt
10. admit
11. relaxation
12. whole
13. lazy
14. partial
15. deceitful
16. stiff
17. divide
18. common
19. abandon
20. modern

Antonyms: Exercise 4 (p. 54)

1. wrong
2. murmur
3. goodness
4. folly
5. unworthy
6. repulsive
7. divided
8. something
9. aged
10. deny
11. good

Answer Keys

12. incomplete
13. stand
14. square
15. silent
16. benevolence
17. assist
18. sin
19. humility
20. surrender

Antonyms: Exercise 5 (p. 55)

Antonyms: Exercise 9 (p. 59)

1. yes
2. yes
3. no
4. no
5. yes
6. yes
7. no
8. no
9. yes
10. yes
11. yes
12. no
13. yes
14. yes
15. no
16. no
17. yes
18. yes
19. yes
20. yes
21. yes
22. no
23. yes
24. no
25. no
26. no
27. yes
28. yes
29. yes
30. yes

Antonyms: Exercise 10 (p. 60)

1. no
2. yes
3. yes
4. no
5. yes
6. yes
7. yes
8. yes
9. no
10. yes
11. yes
12. yes
13. no
14. yes
15. yes
16. yes
17. yes
18. no
19. yes
20. yes
21. no
22. yes
23. yes
24. no

25. yes
26. yes
27. yes
28. no
29. yes
30. yes

Antonyms: Exercise 11 (p. 61)

1. no
2. yes
3. yes
4. yes
5. yes
6. no
7. yes
8. yes
9. yes
10. yes
11. no
12. yes
13. yes
14. yes
15. yes
16. yes
17. no
18. yes
19. no
20. yes
21. no
22. yes
23. no
24. yes
25. no
26. yes
27. yes
28. yes
29. no
30. no

Antonyms: Exercise 12 (p. 62)

1. nervous
2. peace
3. even
4. guilty
5. there
6. rare
7. queen
8. single
9. fake
10. noisy
11. below
12. raw
13. defeat
14. solid
15. seek

Antonyms: Exercise 13 (p. 63)

1. those
2. lend
3. go
4. cold
5. present
6. listen
7. slow
8. defend
9. forget

10. polite
11. tight
12. give
13. answer
14. interesting
15. invisible

Antonyms: Exercise 14 (p. 64)

1. sad
2. East
3. right
4. serious
5. thin
6. sharp
7. careful
8. dirty
9. sunny
10. sour
11. quiet
12. dangerous
13. heavy
14. straight
15. open

Antonyms: Exercise 15 (p. 65)

1. lost
2. wild
3. cruel
4. building
5. most
6. queen
7. sunny
8. younger
9. raw
10. repaired
11. strongest
12. valuable
13. tell
14. interesting
15. thickest

Antonyms: Exercise 16 (p. 66)

1. brave
2. succeed
3. joy
4. work
5. like
6. raise

7. future
8. shallow
9. under
10. wrong
11. inner
12. rarely
13. dawn
14. many
15. South

Antonyms: Exercise 17 (p. 67)

1. poor
2. mother
3. beginning
4. discard
5. accepted
6. clean
7. country
8. thankful
9. added
10. specific
11. morning
12. sharp
13. some
14. knowledge
15. noon

Antonyms: Exercise 18 (p. 68)

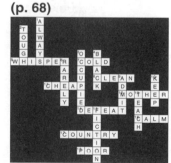

Antonyms: Exercise 21 (p. 71)

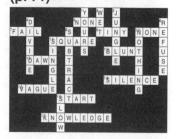

Answer Keys

Synonyms & Antonyms

Antonyms: Exercise 22 (p. 72)

1. b   6. a
2. a   7. b
3. c   8. b
4. a   9. a
5. c   10. b

Antonyms: Exercise 23 (p. 73)

1. a   6. c
2. b   7. a
3. c   8. c
4. a   9. a
5. b   10. b

Antonyms: Exercise 24 (p. 74)

1. b   6. b
2. a   7. c
3. b   8. a
4. c   9. c
5. a   10. b

Antonyms: Exercise 28 (p. 78)

advantage:	disadvantage
	handicap
empty:	full
	occupied
neat:	sloppy
	messy
under:	above
	over
perfectly:	badly
	poorly
ask:	answer
	respond
soft:	rough
	hard
leave:	arrive
	remain
fear:	bravery
	courage
bumpy:	smooth
	flat
heavy:	buoyant
	light
prevent:	aid
	help

false:	true
	faithful
receive:	abandon
	discard
many:	few
	meager

Antonyms: Exercise 29 (p. 79)

victory:	loss
	defeat
tall:	stubby
	short
colorful:	colorless
	pale
over:	beneath
	under
rude:	mannerly
	polite
round:	straight
	square
vague:	specific
	certain
clean:	dirty
	soiled
equal:	uneven
	irregular
ignorant:	intelligent
	aware
kind:	cruel
	rough
remember:	ignore
	forget
question:	reply
	answer
peace:	conflict
	war
dark:	light
	bright

Antonyms: Exercise 30 (p. 80)

discard:	keep
	retain
work:	leisure
	play
stern:	kind
	gentle
shallow:	deep
	bottomless

quiet:	loud
	noisy
little:	big
	large
create:	destroy
	ruin
damage:	fix
	repair
early:	late
	tardy
enemy:	ally
	friend
light:	weighty
	heavy
often:	rarely
	seldom
difficult:	easy
	simple
tender:	tough
	hard
cheap:	costly
	expensive

Antonyms: Exercise 32 (p. 82)

1. A, arrival, departure
2. S, annoy, irritate
3. S, look, observe
4. S, broke, shattered
5. A, big, little
6. A, genuine, fake
7. S, pretty, beautiful
8. S, careful, cautious
9. S, edge, border
10. A, catches, releases
11. A, thick, thin
12. S, yell, shout
13. A, under, over
14. A, those, these
15. A, yours, mine
16. A, leave, retrieve
17. A, close, open
18. S, call, phone
19. A, forget, remember
20. S, hurry, rush

Antonyms: Exercise 33 (p. 83)

1. S, tired, weary
2. S, buy, purchase
3. A, solid, liquid
4. A, calm, nervous
5. S, fearless, brave
6. S, abroad, overseas
7. S, entry, door
8. S, easy, simple
9. A, cooked, raw
10. A, king, queen
11. A, hide, seek
12. S, finish, end
13. S, pile, heap
14. S, cool, frosty
15. S, scream, shriek
16. A, stop, go
17. A, see, hear
18. A, friendly, grumpy
19. S, trap, cage
20. S, open, unlocked